A COOK'S TOUR OF THE ROM

The ROM Reproductions Association
Royal Ontario Museum

A COOK'S TOUR OF THE ROM
by
The ROM Reproductions Association

Second Edition, First Printing — April 1990

Copyright © 1990 by
The ROM Reproductions Association
Royal Ontario Museum
100 Queen's Park
Toronto, Ontario
Canada   M5S 2C6

Canadian Cataloguing in Publication Data

Main entry under title:
A Cook's tour of the ROM

Rev. ed. —

Coordinators: Barbara Ann Hynes, Barbara Hill.
ISBN 0-919845-82-7

1. Cookery International.   2. Royal Ontario
Museum.   1. Hynes, Barbara-Ann.   II. Hill,
Barbara.   III. ROM Reproductions Association.

TX725.A1C66   1990   641.5'9   C90-097058-8

Illustrations by:
Ruth Storie
Toronto, Ontario

Designed, Printed and Produced in Canada by:
Centax Books, a Division of M•C•Graphics Inc.
Publishing Director: Margo Embury
1048 Fleury Street, Regina, Saskatchewan, Canada   S4N 4W8
(306) 359-3737 / 359-7580
Fax (306) 525-3955

THE COMMITTEE

"A Cook's Tour of the ROM" was first published in 1978 by the Members' Volunteer Committee of the Royal Ontario Museum. This second, revised edition is published by The ROM Reproductions Association. The Association arranges for the manufacture of reproductions and adaptations of ROM artifacts for sale in the ROM Reproductions Shop which is a project of the Members' Volunteer Committee. All profits from the Shop go to enrich the collections of the Museum.

The Cookbook Committee consists of Mary Bosley, Barbara Hill, Barbara Ann Hynes, Evelyn Meagher, Joan Robson, Margaret Simpson, Ruth Storie and Pauline Toker.

INTRODUCTION

The collections of the Royal Ontario Museum embrace "the arts of man through all the years", and you could easily argue that the earliest art was the preparation of food. It has always been characteristic of humanity to improve and embellish what begins as a necessity and elevate it into an art which enhances life. The Museum galleries are rich in objects related to the vital art of cooking — from the primitive to the most sophisticated.

In this cookbook we offer a few menus and recipes that reflect some of the major cultures represented in the collections. The recipes are intended only to convey the spirit of regional cooking, adapted to North American tastes.

Because the pleasure of sharing meals with friends is increased if the ambience is appealing, we have also ventured to suggest decorative themes that evoke the atmosphere of the countries chosen. The feeling of place can be captured by a happy marriage of table setting and food. Accessories need not, of course, be of "museum quality", but their shapes and colours should create the desired mood. Objects from around the world are available in many shops today and, what is more, a second look in your own storage cupboards can often give you ideas for putting old possessions to new uses.

Our "Cook's Tour" also lures you into the galleries to discover some of the interesting objects related to food and drink. Similar things may be seen in other museums of the world, and a cook's-eye view of gallery visiting provides a different but fascinating approach. We hope, therefore, that this cookbook will please the eye, the mind and the palate.

TABLE OF CONTENTS

TABLE OF CONTENTS

CANADA

Drawing of Mallorytown glass
pitcher, of free-blown aquamarine glass
with applied lily-pad decoration.
Attributed to the Mallorytown Glass Works,
Mallorytown, Upper Canada, the earliest
known glass factory in Canada, circa
1839-40. Royal Ontario Museum
957.53.2.
This pitcher has been reproduced by
Jamie Sherman for
ROM Reproductions.

CANADA

Canada's forests have always been one of her greatest natural resources and throughout the history of the country many beautiful and practical things have been made of wood. The Northwest Coast Indians, who lived in the shadow of the giant cedars of British Columbia, became very skilled woodworkers. They developed one of the most elaborate of all native Canadian cultures, because the climate and relative ease of food gathering allowed them considerable leisure. They lived in settled communities near the Pacific, with its plentiful salmon, and made permanent homes out of cedar planks. They were expert carvers of totem poles, decorative houseposts, and all sorts of domestic equipment.

Animals had a special significance in this society, so that many of the household objects display animal carvings. A tribe was divided into clans, which associated themselves with a family or clan totem, usually an animal or a bird that legend had connected in a special way to a particular family. In the collections of the Department of Ethnology is a dish with a carved bear's head, the totem of the bear people. Another dish is carved and painted to resemble a long-billed bird with a frog on its tail. A wonderful ladle is in the form of a beaver. The wide flat tail is the handle; the body is scooped out to create the bowl and the face, with teeth bared, decorates the tip of the bowl.

The collections of the Canadian Decorative Arts Department attest that the early European settlers also made use of the trees to produce a wide variety of treenware, small wooden objects for domestic and farm use. Bowls, scoops, paddles and rolling pins, which were strictly functional, were seldom decorated. However, carved patterns appear on butter prints and maple sugar moulds, of which there is a delightful collection. Popular designs were hearts, animals and fish, leaves and flowers.

In the early spring, the best loaves of maple sugar were set aside for Christmas. A "house" mould made in Quebec and a sample of the finished product revive happy childhood memories.

The Canadiana glass collection, with its comprehensive range of utilitarian objects made for 19th- and early 20th-century homes also arouses nostalgia. Grandmother's quart sealers and pressed glass tableware are now treasures to many collectors. One interesting item is an early soda bottle. It was made with a rounded bottom to reduce the stress of the bubbly liquid (early bottles were not as strong as those of today). Soft drinks were sold in the streets from carts packed with straw to hold the bottles upright. The buyer brought his or her own cup or container and after dispensing the liquid into it, returned the bottle to the vendor — an early example of recycling.

THANKSGIVING IN THE COUNTRY

Thanksgiving is a wonderful time of the year when the countryside is ablaze with colour and markets overflow with the fruits of the season. It is a time for gatherings of families and friends. Festive meals attractively presented add to the spirit of the occasion.

Ideas for table decorations may be borrowed from our pioneer ancestors. Quilts make stunning tablecloths, as do round hooked mats. Decoys with an arrangement of dried grasses and moss create an effective centrepeice. Another seasonal and appropriate table decoration is a wooden salad bowl filled with gourds, Indian corn and bittersweet.

Serves 8

Baked Peameal or Smoked Canadian Bacon
with Cumberland Sauce
Cheese Puff
or
Spinach Casserole
Salad of Assorted Greens
with
Lemon Chive Dressing
Melon
Pecan Cookies

BAKED PEAMEAL OR SMOKED CANADIAN BACON

2½-3 lb.	piece peameal or smoked Canadian bacon	1.25-1.5 kg
2 cups	apple juice	500 mL
½ cup	brown sugar	125 mL
1 tsp.	dry mustard	5 mL
	vinegar	

Place the bacon in a baking dish and add apple juice to a depth of about 1" (2.5 cm). Bake, uncovered, at 325°F (160°C) for approximately 1½ hours. Baste occasionally with the juice; add more juice if needed.

Combine sugar, mustard and just enough vinegar to make a smooth paste. Remove the bacon from the oven, coat the top and sides with the sugar paste, and return it to the oven for a further 15 minutes.

CUMBERLAND SAUCE

1 tsp.	dry mustard	5 mL
¼ tsp.	powdered cloves	1 mL
¼ tsp.	powdered cinnamon	1 mL
2 tbsp.	cider or malt vinegar	30 mL
2 tbsp.	port wine	30 mL
½	orange, juice and grated rind	½
6 oz.	crab apple or red currant jelly	170 mL

Combine all the ingredients in a saucepan. Heat the mixture just enough to blend in the spices and partly melt the jelly.

Cheese Puff

6 tbsp.	butter	90 mL
8 slices	white bread, cubed	8
8	eggs	8
2 cups	milk	500 mL
	salt and pepper to taste	
1 cup	grated sharp Cheddar cheese	250 mL
½ cup	coarsely chopped sweet peppers, fresh or preserved	125 mL

Heat the butter and sauté the bread cubes in it. Spread the cubes over the bottom of a greased 9 x 13" (22 x 33 cm) baking dish. Beat the eggs until they are light; add the milk, salt and pepper and mix well. Sprinkle the grated cheese over the bread cubes and then the peppers over the cheese. Pour the egg mixture over the peppers. Refrigerate for several hours or overnight. Bake, uncovered, at 325°F (160°C) for 45 minutes.

Spinach Casserole

2 lbs.	fresh spinach, or 2 x 10 oz. (284 mL) packages frozen	1 kg
	salt to taste	
2 cups	creamed cottage cheese	500 mL
4	eggs, beaten	4
2 tsp.	seasoned salt	10 mL
½ tsp.	pepper	2 mL
dash	nutmeg	dash
½ cup	grated Cheddar cheese	125 mL
4 tbsp.	chopped almonds	60 mL
	paprika to taste	

Cook the spinach in lightly salted water until it is barely tender, about 5 minutes. Drain it, chop finely, and put it in a bowl. Add the salt, cottage cheese, eggs, seasoned salt, pepper and nutmeg, and mix well. Put the mixture in a 2-quart (2 L) ovenproof casserole and sprinkle with the Cheddar cheese, almonds and paprika. Bake, uncovered, at 350° (180°C) for about 45 minutes.

SALAD OF ASSORTED GREENS

7 cups	assorted greens (lettuce, endive, watercress, etc.)	1.75 L
½ cup	thinly sliced radish	125 mL
½ cup	thinly sliced green onions	125 mL
½ cup	thinly sliced cucumber	125 mL

Wash greens and dry thoroughly. Tear into bite-sized pieces and put in a large salad bowl with radish, green onion and cucumber slices. Prepare Lemon Chive dressing, below. Add enough dressing to coat greens lightly and toss gently. (This basic salad may be varied by adding sliced celery, peppers, tomatoes, avocado, herbs, etc.)

LEMON CHIVE DRESSING

½ cup	lemon juice	125 mL
2 tsp.	sugar	10 mL
2 tsp.	Dijon-style mustard	10 mL
1 cup	olive oil	250 mL
¼ cup	chopped chives	50 mL
	salt and pepper	

In a bowl, combine the lemon juice, sugar and mustard. Whisk in the olive oil until mixture is smooth. Add the chives and salt and pepper to taste and mix again.

PECAN COOKIES

2½ tbsp.	butter	37 mL
2 cups	brown sugar	500 mL
2	eggs, beaten	2
1 tsp.	vanilla	5 mL
½ cup	cake flour	125 mL
1 tsp.	baking powder	5 mL
1 tsp.	salt	5 mL
1½ cups	coarsely chopped pecans	375 mL

In a mixing bowl, cream the butter and sugar; add the beaten eggs and vanilla. Sift in the combined flour, baking powder and salt. Add the pecans and stir. The batter will be very thin and runny. Drop batter a teaspoonful (5 mL) at a time, onto a greased and floured cookie sheet, preferably Teflon-coated; keep the cookies well separated, only 8 or 9 to a sheet. Bake at 375°F (190°C) for 5 to 7 minutes (remove the cookies before they are brown). Let them cool a little before lifting them from the cookie sheet (too soon and they crumble; too late and they stick and tear). Makes 4 to 5 dozen.

Serves 8

Scalloped Oysters with Toasted Mushroom Rolls
Wild Rice and Shrimp Salad with Curry Dressing
Watercress and Spinach Salad with Creamy Dressing
Cranberry Crumble
or
Fresh Orange Cream

SCALLOPED OYSTERS

4 cups	oysters (2 pints)	1 L
5 tbsp.	chopped onion	75 mL
6 tbsp.	butter, melted	90 mL
6 cups	bread crumbs	1.5 L
4 tbsps.	chopped parsley	60 mL
	salt and pepper to taste	
	Worcestershire sauce to taste	

Drain the oysters and save the liquor. Sauté the onion in 1 tbsp. (15 mL) melted butter until it is soft. Combine the remaining melted butter with the bread crumbs. Spread ¼ of the crumbs in a thin layer over the bottom of a greased shallow casserole, large enough to accommodate the oysters in 2 layers. Cover the crumbs with a layer of oysters. Sprinkle the oysters with half the onion and parsley, salt and pepper to taste and a few drops of Worcestershire sauce. Cover with another layer of crumbs and oysters and sprinkle with the remaining onion and parsley, salt and pepper, and a few drops of Worcestershire sauce. Sprinkle the whole with the oyster liquor and spread the remaining crumbs over the top. Bake, uncovered, at 400°F (200°C) for 30 minutes. Serve immediately.

If serving this dish as a first course, cut the amount of oysters to 3 cups (750 mL) and the buttered crumbs to 4 cups (1 L). Arrange the ingredients in single layers in 8 scallop shells or small ramekins. Bake, uncovered, at 400°F (200°C) for 15 minutes.

TOASTED MUSHROOMS ROLLS

¼ cup	butter	50 mL
½ lb.	mushrooms, finely chopped	250 g
3 tbsp.	flour	45 mL
½ tsp.	salt	2 mL
1 cup	light cream	250 mL
2 tsp.	minced chives	10 mL
1 tsp.	lemon juice	5 mL
1	large loaf fresh bread, thinly sliced	1

Melt the butter and sauté the mushrooms in it for 5 minutes. Blend in the flour and salt and then stir in the cream. Cook and stir the mixture until it is thick. Add the chives and the lemon juice and stir. Remove the mixture from the stove and allow it to cool.

Remove the crusts from the bread. Spread each slice with a thin layer of the mushroom mixture and roll it up. Cut the rolls in half and arrange them on a lightly greased cookie sheet. Bake at 400°F (200°C) for about 10 to 15 minutes, turning the rolls when the tops are toasted. The mushroom rolls may be made at any time and frozen. Defrost them before toasting.

WILD RICE AND SHRIMP SALAD

2-3 tbsp.	olive oil	30-45 mL
½ lb.	fresh mushrooms, sliced	250 g
½ lb.	raw shrimp, peeled	250 g
½ lb.	wild rice, cooked and cooled	250 g
3	hard-cooked eggs, diced	3
	salt and pepper to taste	
	Curry Dressing, recipe follows	

Heat the oil and sauté the mushrooms in it for about 5 minutes. Remove the mushrooms. Add the raw shrimp and sauté for another 5 minutes, or until the shrimp are cooked. Remove from heat. Place the cooked rice in a large bowl. Add the mushrooms, shrimp and diced eggs. Mix gently and season with salt and pepper. Pour ¼ cup (50 mL) of Curry Dressing into the shrimp and rice mixture and combine gently. Serve the rest of the dressing in a separate bowl.

CURRY DRESSING

⅛ tsp.	dried oregano	0.5 mL
⅛ tsp.	dried thyme	0.5 mL
2 tsp.	curry powder	10 mL
1	garlic clove, mashed	1
8	green onions, finely chopped	8
4 tbsp.	lemon juice	60 mL
1 cup	sour cream	250 mL
1 cup	mayonnaise	250 mL
	salt and pepper	

Combine all ingredients thoroughly.

WATERCRESS AND SPINACH SALAD

1	bunch spinach, thoroughly washed, dried and crisped	1
2-3	bunches watercress, processed as above Creamy Dressing, recipe follows	2-3

Remove stems from spinach and tear into bite-sized pieces. Remove the large stems from the watercress to make short sprays. Allow a handful of prepared greens per person. Combine the greens in a salad bowl, add Creamy Dressing to taste and toss until it is all lightly coated.

CREAMY DRESSING

1 tsp.	salt	5 mL
1 tsp.	pepper	5 mL
1 tsp.	Dijon-style mustard	5 mL
½ tsp.	dry mustard	2 mL
½ tsp.	lemon juice or more	2 mL
2 tbsp.	tarragon vinegar	30 mL
¼ cup	olive oil	50 mL
½ cup	vegetable oil	125 mL
⅓ cup	18% cream (coffee cream)	75 mL
3 tbsp.	fresh basil OR 1 tbsp. (15 mL) dried	45 mL

Blend the above ingredients with a wire whisk or in a blender or food processor. Keeps well in the refrigerator.

CRANBERRY CRUMBLE

1 cup	quick-cooking oats	250 mL
½ cup	flour	125 mL
1 cup	brown sugar	250 mL
½ cup	butter	125 mL
2 cups	whole cranberry sauce	500 mL

Combine the oats, flour, sugar and butter to form a crumbly mixture. Spread half of the mixture in an 8" (20 cm) square pan. Cover it with the cranberry sauce and spread the remaining oatmeal mixture over the top. Bake at 350°F (180°C) for about 45 minutes. Serve the crumble hot with cream or ice cream.

FRESH ORANGE CREAM

2 cups	freshly squeezed orange juice	500 mL
1	orange, grated rind of	1
½ cup	sugar	125 mL
1 cup	water	250 mL
3 tbsp.	cornstarch	45 mL
1 tbsp.	butter	15 mL
2	egg whites	2

Combine all the ingredients, except the egg whites, in the top of a double boiler and cook, stirring constantly, until the mixture is thickened and no raw starch taste remains, about 20 minutes. Allow the mixture to cool. Beat the egg whites until stiff, but not dry, and gently fold them into the orange cream mixture. Pour the fresh orange cream into a glass bowl and refrigerate.

DINNER

Serves 8

Zucchini Soup
or
Nova Scotia Scallops
Roast Wild Duck
or
Casserole of Duck À L'Orange with Orange Sauce
Butternut Squash with Cheese and Cream
Braised Pearl Onions
Apple Crisp

ZUCCHINI SOUP

¼ cup	butter	50 mL
1 cup	sliced onion or leeks	250mL
4 cups	diced unpeeled zucchini	1 L
¼ cup	parsley	50 mL
3 cups	chicken broth	750 mL
1 cup	milk	250 mL
1 cup	heavy cream	250 mL
	salt and pepper to taste	
3 tbsp.	chopped chives	45 mL
1	lemon, thinly sliced	1

Melt the butter and gently cook onion or leeks in it, in a covered pan, until the vegetables are transparent. Add the zucchini, parsley and chicken broth and simmer until the vegetables are tender. Purée in a food processor or blender. Add milk, cream, salt and pepper. The soup may be served hot or cold, garnished with chopped chives and a lemon slice.

Nova Scotia Scallops

2 lbs.	scallops	1 kg
	flour to coat scallops	
2 tbsp.	butter	30 mL
2 tbsp.	oil or more	30 mL
	salt and pepper	
1 cup	finely chopped parsley	250 mL
1	garlic clove, minced (optional)	1
2	lemons, cut in wedges	2

Rinse the scallops and dry them. Place the scallops on a board and cut them in halves if they are small or in quarters if they are large. Place them in a paper bag with the flour and shake until all the scallops are coated. Brush off any excess flour. Put the butter and oil in a large frying pan and heat until it is sizzling. Add the scallops and cook over moderate heat for 5 to 10 minutes, or until the scallops begin to brown. Add the parsley and garlic and stir the mixture for 2 minutes. Serve immediately with lemon wedges.

Roast Wild Duck

4	wild ducks	4
4	apples	4
	butter	
	orange liqueur	
2	oranges, sliced	2

Clean and prepare ducks. Put a whole apple inside each duck and rub the outside of the bird with butter. Roast in a covered pan for 3 hours at 325°F (160°C), basting occasionally with orange liqueur. Remove the lid for the last half hour. Serve decorated with orange slices.

Casserole Of Duck À L'orange

4	domestic ducks	4
¼ cup	butter	50 mL
2	oranges, grated rind of	2
2 cups	orange juice	500 mL
1 tsp.	cinnamon	5 mL
1 tsp.	cloves	5 mL
	salt to taste	
½ tsp.	pepper	2 mL

Cut the ducks into serving pieces. Melt the butter in a heavy casserole, add the duck, and brown the pieces, turning them as necessary so that they brown all over. Add the orange rind, orange juice, cinnamon, cloves, salt and pepper, and stir well. Cover the casserole and cook on top of the stove over low heat until the duck is tender, about 1½ hours. Remove the duck to a warmed dish and serve with Orange Sauce, recipe follows.

Orange Sauce

¼ cup	butter	50 mL
	livers from 4 ducks	
½ tsp	minced garlic	2 mL
¼ cup	flour	50 mL
4 tbsp.	grated orange rind	60 mL
1 tsp.	ketchup	5 mL
¾ cup	orange juice	175 mL
1½ cups	chicken broth	375 mL
⅓ cup	red wine	75 mL
⅓ cup	orange marmalade	75 mL
4	large navel oranges, peeled and sectioned	4
	salt and pepper to taste	

In a saucepan melt the butter. Add the livers and gently brown them. Add the garlic and cook 2 to 3 minutes. Remove the pan from the heat. Take the livers out of the pan, chop them finely and set them aside. Return the pan to the stove and add the flour, orange rind and ketchup. Stir the mixture until it is smooth. Gradually add the orange juice, broth, wine and marmalade and bring the mixture to boiling point. Reduce the heat and simmer, stirring constantly, for 15 minutes. Add the orange sections, chopped livers, salt and pepper.

Butternut Squash With
Cheese And Cream

2	medium butternut squash (about 5 pounds [2.2 kg] total)	2
	salt and pepper to taste	
8 oz.	Gruyère cheeese, grated	250 g
2 cups	10% cream (half & half cream)	500 mL

Peel and seed the squash and cut them into slices about ¼" (1 cm) thick. (A food processor is ideal for slicing.) Spread the slices in layers in a shallow buttered 9" x 13" (4 L) casserole, seasoning each layer with salt and pepper. Spread the cheese over the squash. Scald the cream and pour it over the casserole. Bake, uncovered, at 350°F (180°C) for about 40 minutes, or until the squash is tender. More scalded cream may be added to the casserole if it seems to be getting dry as it cooks.

Braised Pearl Onions

3 pints	small white onions (1" [2.5 cm] or less)	1.5 L
1 cup	chicken stock	250 mL
2 tbsp.	butter	30 mL
	salt and pepper	
3 tbsp.	chopped parsley	45 mL

Cover the onions with boiling water and let stand for 3 minutes. Drain and rinse in cold water. Cut off ends and peel. Simmer the onions in stock for 30-45 minutes, until tender. Most of the liquid will be absorbed. Drain, if necessary, and dress with butter, salt, pepper and parsley.

6-8	large cooking apples (Cortland, Spy, or Blenheim Orange)	6-8
¼ tsp.	cinnamon	1 mL
	pinch of salt	
1 tsp.	lemon juice	5 mL
¼ cup	orange juice	50 mL
¼ cup	all-purpose flour	50 mL
¾ cup	quick-cooking oats	175 mL
1 cup	brown sugar	250mL
½ cup	butter	125 mL

Pare and core the apples and slice them into a bowl. Add the cinnamon, salt and lemon juice, and toss. Put the apples in a buttered casserole and pour the orange juice over them. In a separate bowl, mix the flour, oats and sugar. Cut in the butter until the mixture is crumbly. Spread the crumb mixture over the apples and bake, uncovered, at 350°F (180°C) for 30 minutes, or until the apples are tender. (A recipe for an alternative topping, Brandied Pecan, follows.)

If apple crisp is served hot, a sauce of sour cream mixed with grated lemon or orange rind makes an agreeable accompaniment. If it is served cold, cream or vanilla ice cream are pleasant additions.

Apple Crisp is a dessert that can be made in the autumn when apples are at their best and stored in the freezer. Store uncooked and well-wrapped.

BRANDIED PECAN TOPPING

½ cup	brown sugar	125 mL
½ cup	all-purpose flour	125 mL
1 tsp.	crushed coriander seeds	5 mL
1½ tsp.	cinnamon	7 mL
½ cup	butter	125 mL
1 cup	chopped pecans or walnuts	250 mL
¼ cup	brandy (optional)	50 mL

Mix the dry ingredients, except the nuts, in a bowl, and work the butter into them until the mixture resembles coarse meal. Add the chopped nuts and stir. Spread the crumb mixture over the apples and baked, uncovered, at 350°F (180°C) for 30 minutes, or until the apples are tender. As soon as the apple crisp comes out of the oven, sprinkle the brandy over it.

DINNER

Serves 8

Cream of Pumpkin Soup
Roast Pork Tenderloin with Madeira and Mushroom Sauce
Hot Fruit Compôte
Broccoli
Stuffed Baked Potatoes
Frozen Maple Mousse
Oatmeal Lace Cookies

CREAM OF PUMPKIN SOUP

2 tbsp.	butter or margarine	30 mL
2	medium onions, thinly sliced	2
1 tbsp.	flour	15 mL
2½ cups	chicken stock	625 mL
3 cups	fresh or canned pumpkin purée	750 mL
2 cups	milk	500 mL
1 cup	light cream	250 mL
1 tsp.	salt	5 mL
½ tsp.	pepper	2 mL
¼ tsp.	ginger	1 mL
⅛ tsp.	cinnamon	0.5 mL

In a large saucepan, melt the butter or margarine and sauté the onions in it for 10 minutes, or until they are tender. Remove from heat. Stir the flour into the onion and then gradually stir in 1½ cups (375 mL) of chicken stock. Return the pan to the stove and bring the mixture to a boil. Reduce heat and simmer, covered, for 10 minutes. Ladle the mixture into a blender or food processor. Blend it at high speed until it is completely smooth. Return the mixture to the saucepan and smoothly blend in the pumpkin with a wire whisk. Add the milk, cream, the second cup (250 mL) of the chicken stock and the seasonings; beat with a wire whisk. Heat the soup slowly over medium heat until it is just boiling. Serve hot.

Roast Pork Tenderloin

4 tbsp.	butter	60 mL
4 tbsp.	minced onion	60 mL
3 cups	soft bread crumbs	750 mL
¼ tsp.	savory	1 mL
	salt and pepper to taste	
4	strips pork tenderloin, about ¾ lb. (365 g) each	4
	bacon strips, optional	

Melt the butter in a skillet and cook the onion in it until it is transparent. Add the bread crumbs and mix lightly. Add the seasonings and mix again. (Your own favourite bread stuffing may be substituted for this basic recipe.)

Make several lengthwise cuts in each tenderloin to open them up; spread and flatten slightly. Stuff and tie each pair. Place the tenderloins in a baking dish and cover them with bacon strips if there is no fat. Roast, uncovered, at 350°F (180°C) for about 1 hour. Serve with Madeira and Mushroom Sauce, recipe follows.

Madeira And Mushroom Sauce

2 tbsp.	butter	30 mL
2 tbsp.	minced shallots or scallions	30 mL
2 tbsp.	flour	30 mL
1½ cups	beef broth	375 mL
1 tbsp.	butter	15 mL
¼ lb.	mushrooms, sliced	125 g
½ cup	Madeira	125 mL
	salt and pepper to taste	

Melt the butter in a saucepan and sauté the shallots in it. Blend in the flour and add the broth gradually, stirring until the sauce is smooth. Cook until the sauce thickens, stirring constantly, and then lower the heat and simmer for 10 minutes. Melt 1 tbsp. (15 mL) butter in a small frying pan; add mushrooms and sauté. Add the Maderia and mushrooms to the sauce, simmer for 5 minutes and season.

HOT FRUIT COMPÔTE

19 oz.	can applesauce	540 mL
1 tsp.	cinnamon	5 mL
½ tsp.	ginger	2 mL
½ tsp.	nutmeg	2 mL
½	lemon, juice and grated rind	½
14 oz.	can sliced peaches, drained	398 mL
14 oz.	can sliced pears, drained	398 mL
14 oz.	can diced pineapple, drained	398 mL

Put the applesauce in a 2-quart (2 L) casserole, add the spices and lemon juice and rind, and mix well. Mix in the fruits. Bake, covered, at 250°F (120°C) for at least 1 hour. The longer the compote bakes, the better it is. Serve hot with roast pork.

Pitted Bing cherries and halves of seeded grapes may be added or substituted for peaches, pears and pineapple.

STUFFED BAKED POTATOES

8	baking potatoes, unpeeled but with skins well-scrubbed	8
½ cup	butter	125 mL
¾-1 cup	light cream	175-250 mL
½-1 tsp.	sage	2-5 mL
	salt and pepper to taste	

Bake the potatoes at 400°F (200°C) for about 60 minutes, or until they are soft. Split them in half lengthwise. Scoop out the potatoes, being careful not to break the skins, put potato pulp in a bowl, and mash it well. Add the butter and cream and mix or beat until the potato is fluffy. Season it with sage, salt and pepper. Repack the half-shells, mounding the potato slightly. Return the potato halves to the oven until they are reheated and the tops are lightly browned. The broiler may be used for browning. Stuffed baked potatoes may be prepared ahead of time and refrigerated. They should be removed from the refrigerator 1 hour before reheating.

FROZEN MAPLE MOUSSE

4	egg yolks, well-beaten	4
1 cup	maple syrup	250 mL
4	egg whites, well-beaten	4
2 cups	heavy cream, whipped	500 mL
¾ cup	chopped pecans	175 mL

Place the egg yolks and maple syrup in the top of a double boiler, over gently boiling water and cook for 5 minutes. Cool and fold in the beaten egg whites, whipped cream and pecans. Transfer the mousse to an ice-cube tray or other suitable container and freeze. Serve in a well-chilled bowl.

OATMEAL LACE COOKIES

½ cup	flour	125 mL
¼ tsp.	baking powder	1 mL
½ cup	sugar	125 mL
½ cup	quick-cooking oats	125 mL
2 tbsp.	heavy cream	30 mL
2 tbsp.	light corn syrup	30 mL
⅓ cup	melted butter or margarine	75 mL
1 tbsp.	vanilla	15 mL

Sift the combined flour, baking powder and sugar into a bowl. Add the oats, cream, corn syrup, butter and vanilla. Mix until the ingredients are well-blended. Drop the batter a half-teaspoon (2 mL) at a time onto an ungreased baking sheet. Keep the spoonfuls 4" (10 cm) apart. Bake in a preheated oven at 350°F (180°C) for 8 to 10 minutes, or until the cookies are lightly browned. Let the cookies stand a few seconds before lifting them from the sheet. Makes 6 dozen 2" (5 cm) cookies.

Jour De L'an

Arranger des brins de pin, de sapin ou de genévrier le long de la table, au centre, en forme de guirlande, comme illustré ci-dessus. Y entremettre des pommes de pin, des mandarines, des pommes rouges et des noix dorées. Le soir, des bougies ajouteraient un effet intéressant.

New Year's Day In Quebec

Along the centre of your dining table arrange short pieces of juniper, spruce, or pine boughs to make a garland something like the one illustrated. Among the boughs tuck pine cones, rosy apples, tangerines, and gilded walnuts. Fat candles or vigil lights placed at intervals are effective for an evening party.

Jour De L'an Au Québec

Déjeuner Ou Souper

Pour 8 personnes

Longe de Porc Frais
Graisse de Rôti
Fèves Vertes Vinaigrette
Pommes de Terre Rissolées
Pudding Glacé

Graisse De Rôti

En achetant la longe de porc, tâchez d'obtenir du boucher un morceau de couenne — vous obtiendrez une plus belle graisse. Une fois la longe cuite, déposez la dans un plat et laissez la refroidir. Aux jus dans la rôtissoire, ajoutez assez d'eau pour avoir environ 1 et ¾ tasse (425 mL) de sauce. Chauffez en grattant le fond et les côtes jusqu'à ce que la sauce soit brune. Ajoutez alors une enveloppe de gélatine (7 g) gonflée dans ¼ tasse (50 mL) d'eau froide. Brassez à feu moyen jusqu'à ce que la gelatine soit fondue. Passez votre moule ou ramequins à l'eau froide et versez-y la sauce. Laissez prendre à la température de la piece (4 à 5 heures, ou toute la nuit), ensuite réfrigérez. Démoulez et servez avec le porc frais, ou encore avec du pain français ou des toasts.

Fèves Vertes Vinaigrette

2 lbs.	fèves vertes	1 kg
¾ tasse	huile d'olive ou végétale	175 mL
6 c.tb.	vinaigre de vin	90 mL
1	oignon moyen, haché fin	1
1 c.t.	sel	5 mL
	poivre fraîchement moulu	
	basilic	

Faire cuire les fèves al dente. Egoutter. Faire la vinaigrette avec l'huile, le vinaigre, l'oignon et les épices. Verser sur les fèves une heure avant de servir. Les servir chambrées.

POMMES DE TERRE RISSOLÉES

3 c.tb.	beurre	45 mL
2 c.tb.	farine	30 mL
3 tasses	lait	750 mL
3 tasses	pommes de terre rapées, crues	750 mL
1	oignon moyen râpé	1
	sel	
	poivre fraîchement moulu	
2 c.tb.	beurre	30 mL

Faire chauffer le four à 325°F (160°C).

Faire fondre 3 c.tb. (45 mL) beurre dans une casserole. Y ajoutez la farine, brasser et laisser mijoter un peu. Enlever du feu, ajouter peu à peu le lait, bien brasser. Remettre sur un feu moyen et cuire, tout en brassant, jusqu'à ce que la sauce blanche soit légèrement épaissie. Y ajouter sans tarder les pommes de terre, l'oignon, et sel et poivre au gout. Verser dans un plant allant au four, peu profond, 13" x 9½" x 2" (33 x 23 x 5 cm). Parsemer de beurre et cuire au four, à découvert, 2 heures. Les pommes de terre seront tendres, et le dessus croustillant.

PUDDING GLACÉ

12 gros	macarons ou 36 petits	12
¾ tasse	sherry	175 mL
3 tasses	crème 35%	750 mL
¾ tasse	sucre	175 mL
1½ c.t.	de vanille	7 mL
¾ lb.	cerises confites	365 g

Faire tremper les macarons émiettés dans le sherry. Battre la crème, y ajouter sucre et vanille. Chemiser le moule avec crème fouettée et mettre cerises autour du moule et les macarons écrasés au centre. Couvrir de crème fouettée et recommencer avec cerises et macarons. Finir en couvrant de crème. Refroidir le moule avant de le remplir.

Mettre au congélateur quelques jours avant de servir.

NOTE: Cette recette sert 16 à 18 personnes et nécessite un moule de 8 à 10 tasses (2-2.5 mL).

Pour 8 personnes, diviser en 2 moules, et en garder un pour une autre occasion.

New Year's Day In Quebec

───── Dinner Or Supper ─────

Serves 8

Cold Loin of Pork
with Graisse de Rôti
Green Beans Vinaigrette
Shirred Potatoes
Pudding Glacé

Cold Loin Of Pork
───── With Graisse De Rôti ─────

5-6 lbs.	pork loin	2.2-2.5 kg
1 tbsp.	unflavoured gelatin (7 g env.)	15 mL
¼ cup	cold water	50 mL

When buying the loin of pork, ask the butcher for a piece of pork rind, which will add to the flavour. Cook the roast at 350°F (180°C) for 40 to 45 minutes per pound (500 g). Remove to a platter and allow it to cool.

Add water to the juices in the roasting pan to bring the liquid to 1¾ cups (425 mL). Place the pan on top of the stove and stir over medium heat, scraping to loosen the bits stuck to the bottom and sides. When the sauce is brown, add 1 envelope of gelatin soaked in ¼ cup (50 mL) cold water and stir over medium heat until dissolved. Pour into a mould (or individual ramekins), which has been rinsed in cold water. Let set for 4 to 5 hours or overnight at room temperature, and then refrigerate. Unmould and serve with the cold pork. Graisse de Rôti is also delicious spread on French bread or toast.

───── Green Beans Vinaigrette ─────

2 lbs.	fresh green beans	1 kg
6 tbsp.	wine vinegar	90 mL
¾ cup	olive or vegetable oil	175 mL
1	medium onion, finely chopped	1
	freshly ground pepper	
1 tsp.	salt	5 mL
	basil to taste	

Cook the beans until they are tender but still firm. Drain them and place them in a salad bowl. In another bowl thoroughly mix the vinegar, oil, onion and seasonings. Pour the dressing over the beans about 1 hour before serving. Serve at room temperature.

3 tbsp.	butter	45 mL
2 tbsp.	flour	30 mL
3 cups	milk	750 mL
3 cups	grated raw potato	750 mL
1	medium onion, finely grated	1
	salt and freshly ground pepper to taste	
2 tbsp.	butter	30 mL

Melt the 3 tbsp. (45 mL) butter in a saucepan. Sprinkle in the flour, blend and let the mixture bubble up well. Remove the pan from the heat, add the milk gradually and stir to blend. Return the pan to moderate heat and cook the sauce until it thickens slightly, stirring constantly. Immediately add the potatoes, onion, salt and pepper. Pour the mixture into a large shallow baking dish, 13" x 9" x 2" (33 x 23 x 5 cm) and dot the top with butter. Bake, uncovered, at 325°F (160°C) for 2 hours, or until the top is brown and crunchy and the potatoes are tender.

──────── PUDDING GLACÉ ────────

12	large macaroons, or 36 small, crumbled	12
¾ cup	sherry	175 mL
3 cups	whipping cream	750 mL
¾ cup	granulated sugar	175 mL
1½ tsp.	vanilla	7 mL
¾ lb.	glacé cherries	365 g

This recipe serves 16 to 18 and requires an 8-10 cup (2-2.5 L) mould or bowl. To serve 8, divide the pudding into 2 moulds and keep 1 in the freezer for another occasion. Cool the moulds in the refrigerator before filling them.

Soak the crumbled macaroons in the sherry. Whip the cream, adding the sugar and vanilla as you whip. Coat the mould with whipped cream. Arrange a ring of cherries around the bottom edge of the mould and a layer of the crumbled macaroons in the centre. Cover with whipped cream and repeat the layering. Top with whipped cream. Freeze the pudding for a few days before serving.

ENGLAND

Drawing of a fox-mask stirrup cup,
English, probably Derby 1800-1830.
Bone porcelain, naturalistically painted overglaze.
Royal Ontario Museum
985.156.2
Gift of Mr. Jack Ryrie

ENGLAND

Wassail bowls are associated with Christmas, but the origin of the word goes back to Anglo- Saxon times. The word meant "Be Well" and was used when friends gathered to drink to each other's health. Later, hot punch was served from large bowls in the Christmas season, and carollers carried their own wooden bowls from door to door, hoping to be rewarded with a warming drink. There are two such bowls in the collections of the European Department, one rosewood and one mahogany, shaped like oversized goblets. The larger one has a silver plaque with an inscription in Welsh and the English translation: "God Bless all True Brittain's, Health to the Donor". Both date from the seventeenth century. Toast croutons were usually floated in the wassail bowl and were very tasty when well soaked in the hot brew. When drinking someone's health, the bowl was passed around and ended with the person honoured, who got the coveted toast. This is the origin of the expression "to drink a toast".

In the late Middle Ages and early Renaissance, English travellers began to bring back souvenirs from far-off lands. Particularly valued were wonderful natural objects such as ostrich eggs, shells and coconuts which were often believed to have mystical or medicinal properties and to bring good fortune. These treasures were mounted in silver or silver-gilt and turned into vessels, usually for drinking. There is an ostrich-egg cup in the Lee Collection and several examples of coconut cups. The coconut was particularly popular because it was not too fragile and could be polished or carved. These exotic cups were very fashionable in the Tudor period.

Another interesting drinking vessel is the stirrup cup, a footless cup or glass traditionally handed up to a rider in the saddle before the hunt, or to a mounted traveller when he stopped at an inn. The provision of "one for the road", while not recommended for the driver of today, may have supplied much needed warmth and courage to the horseman embarking on an uncomfortable or hazardous journey. Stirrup cups were made in many fanciful shapes, often animals' heads such as fox, deer, hare or doe. One can see an ancient version of such vessels in the Greek Gallery where there are rhytons made in the likenesses of a mule's and a ram's head. The exact origins of these cups are lost in the past, probably coming from nomadic cultures and related to the use of the hunter's horn for refreshment while hunting. In eighteenth century England costly fox-mask cups, handmade in silver, were a luxury for well-to-do hunters. Porcelain, pottery or glass cups were more common at coaching houses and inns. In the collections of the European Department are two examples of Anglo-Irish glass stirrup cups.

In the English Collections there is an intriguing oval covered dish which looks like a pie, charmingly ornamented with acanthus leaves and pie-crust line decoration. Game pies were, for centuries, a vital part of the Englishman's diet, and both meat and fruit pies are still great favourites. The "raised" or free-standing pie of the past was a massive creation. During the Napoleonic Wars a shortage of flour discouraged the making of pastry and the imitation ceramic pie crust was introduced to provide a substitute container for the fillings. Wedgwood perfected the golden-brown stoneware called cane-ware. Glaze was applied to the inside only, and it was used to hold hot food or, sometimes, only for display on the dinner table.

CHRISTMAS IN ENGLAND

Of course you have "decked the hall" in your family's favourite way. For the festive dinner, why not cover the table with a felt cloth in the colour you have chosen for your Christmas decorating scheme? For the centrepiece, make or buy a small tree and decorate it with cookies, tiny candy canes, and miniature brightly wrapped packages.

To make a Christmas tree, you will need a cone of chicken wire and a generous supply of green boughs. Make the cone a little smaller than you wish the finished tree to be, since it will fill out considerably when stuffed with the greenery. Fill the cone with wet oasis (water-absorbent florist's foam). Then, start at the top with a handsome piece of boxwood, spruce, or balsam to establish the height. Cut short lengths of greenery and poke them into the oasis, working down from the top and turning the cone as you descend. A lazy Susan makes an ideal working platform, but a plate will do. The finished tree should be symmetrical and well filled, with no spaces showing. If you keep the oasis damp, the centrepiece will stay fresh through the Twelve Days of Christmas.

For Christmas breakfast, brighten the table with a cloth or runners of chintz in colours that complement the scheme of your room. As a centrepiece, try a silver trophy filled with holly and evergreens.

Serves 8

Wassail Bowl
Plum Tomato Bouillon
or
Smoked Salmon
Garnished with Capers and Lemon Wedges
Braised Pheasant with Liver Stuffing
or
Rock Cornish Hens with Cranberry Glaze
Puréed Peas
Cauliflower with Butter and Parsley
Trifle
or
Mince Tarts
or
Mincemeat Crêpes

———————— WASSAIL BOWL ————————

1 cup	water	250 mL
1 tsp.	ground ginger	5 mL
2"	stick cinnamon	5 cm
6	allspice berries	6
4	cardamom seeds	4
½ tsp.	nutmeg	2 mL
6	whole cloves	6
4	coriander seeds	4
2 pints	ale (32 oz.)	1 L
26 oz. bottle	sweet sherry or Madeira	750 mL
2 cups	sugar	500 mL
6	eggs, separated	6
½ cup	cognac	125 mL
12	spiced crab apples	12

Pour the water into a large pot, add all the spices and bring to a boil. Lower the heat and simmer for 10 minutes. Add the ale, sherry and sugar, and heat but do not boil. Beat the egg yolks until they are pale and the whites until they are stiff. Fold the whites into the yolks. Gradually, strain half the ale and sherry mixture into the eggs. Pour this liquid into a warm punch bowl. Bring the remaining ale and sherry mixture to a boil and strain it into the punch bowl. Add the cognac and crab apples and stir. Serve the wassail hot, before dinner, with salted almonds and cocktail biscuits.

PLUM TOMATO BOUILLON

2 x 28 oz.	tins plum tomatoes	2 x 796 mL
4 cups	chicken stock	1 L
½ cup	dry vermouth	125 mL
2 tsp.	sugar	10mL
	salt and pepper to taste	
½ cup	sour cream	125 mL
1 tsp.	curry powder	5 mL
2 tsp.	finely grated lemon peel	10 mL

In a large saucepan combine the tomatoes and chicken stock. Bring to a boil, reduce the heat and gently simmer for 5 minutes. Transfer to a food mill or sieve and purée. Add the vermouth, sugar, salt and pepper to taste. Combine the sour cream with the curry powder and lemon peel. Serve the soup hot or cold with the sour cream topping.

SMOKED SALMON GARNISHED WITH CAPERS AND LEMON WEDGES

1 lb.	thinly-sliced smoked salmon	500 g
2	lemons, quartered	2
	capers	
	leaf lettuce or parsley	

Arrange the salmon on individual plates. Garnish with lemon quarters, capers and lettuce or parsley.

ROCK CORNISH HENS WITH CRANBERRY GLAZE

8	Rock Cornish hens, thawed, 1 lb. (500 g) each	8
4 tsp.	dried thyme	20 mL
4 tsp.	dried summer savory	20 mL
	salt and pepper	
14 oz.	tin whole cranberry sauce	398 mL
¼ cup	butter	50 mL
¼ cup	concentrated frozen orange juice	50 mL
2 tsp.	finely grated orange rind	10 mL
½ tsp.	dried thyme	2 mL

In each hen, place ½ tsp. (2 mL) each of thyme and summer savory; add salt and pepper. Truss. Place in a pan and sprinkle with salt and pepper. Roast in a 425°F (220°C) oven for 30 minutes. Heat together cranberry sauce, butter, orange juice and rind and ½ tsp. (2 mL) thyme. Pour some over each bird. Lower heat to 350°F (180°C) and continue roasting, basting frequently with the cranberry mixture, until well-browned and drumsticks twist easily at the thigh joint, about a half hour longer. Remove to a heated platter and pour sauce over.

BRAISED PHEASANT

	Liver Stuffing, recipe follows	
4	pheasants	4
¼ cup	olive oil	50 mL
4	carrots, cut in rounds	4
4	small onions	4
2 cups	white wine	500 mL
1 cup	beef or chicken stock	250 mL

Lightly stuff pheasants with Liver Stuffing and truss them. In a skillet, heat olive oil and brown the pheasants. Transfer birds to a large roasting pan. Add carrots, onions and liquid from the skillet. Roast pheasants, covered, at 375°F (190°C) for ½ hour. Reduce oven to 350°F (180°C) and roast for 2-2½ hours. Combine wine and stock and baste the birds with this mixture. Serve pheasants with pan drippings poured over them.

LIVER STUFFING

½ cup	olive oil	125 mL
1 lb.	chicken livers and the pheasant livers	500 g
2	garlic cloves, minced	2
½ tsp.	thyme	2 mL
2½ cups	bread crumbs	625 mL
6 tsp.	soft butter	30 mL
4	eggs, lightly beaten	4
	salt and pepper to taste	

In a skillet heat olive oil and sauté livers, for about 5 minutes. Remove livers from the skillet, chop finely and put them in a bowl. Add garlic, thyme and bread crumbs and mix. Blend in butter, eggs, salt and pepper.

PURÉED PEAS

4	green onions, coarsely chopped	4
4 tsp.	chopped mint	20 mL
2 lbs.	frozen peas	1 kg
1 tsp.	sugar	5 mL
4 tbsp.	butter	60mL
¼ cup	heavy cream	50 mL
	salt and pepper to taste	

Add onions and 2 tsp. (10 mL) of mint to frozen peas and cook according to package instructions. Drain peas well and mash thoroughly, or purée in a blender or food processor. Add remaining mint, the sugar, butter, cream, salt and pepper, and blend thoroughly. Put puréed peas in a baking dish set in a pan of hot water and bake at 325°F (160°C) for 45 minutes to 1 hour, or until heated through.

TRIFLE

1	butter cake (9" [23 cm] square), or 12-oz. (340 g) pound cake (made from a mix)	1
2 oz.	light rum (4 tbsp.) or more to taste	60 mL
3 cups	Custard Sauce, recipe follows	750 mL
	red currant jelly or raspberry or strawberry jam	
¾ cup	slivered almonds, toasted	175 mL
1 cup	heavy cream	250 mL
	sugar	
	vanilla	

Cut the cake into 1½" (2.5 cm) cubes. Layer the cubes in the bottom of a glass dessert bowl. Pour the rum over the cake cubes, turning them gently with a fork to distribute the rum. Pour the Custard Sauce over the cake cubes while the sauce is still warm. Gently work a fork down to the bottom of the dish every few inches, so that the custard seeps through. Tightly cover the bowl and allow the mixture to cool. Refrigerate. Before serving, dot the custard with dollops of jelly or jam. Spread the almonds on a cookie sheet and toast them in the oven at 350°F (180°C) for 10 minutes. Watch the almonds carefully so that they do not overbrown. Whip the cream, adding sugar and vanilla to taste, and spread it over the custard and jelly. Sprinkle the whipped cream with the toasted almond slivers.

CUSTARD SAUCE

4	eggs	4
6 tbsp.	sugar	90 mL
	salt to taste	
3 cups	milk	750 mL
	vanilla	
	nutmeg	

Put the eggs, sugar and salt in a bowl and beat lightly. Scald the milk in the top of a double boiler. Mix a little of the hot milk into the beaten eggs and then stir the egg mixture into the rest of the scalded milk. Cook over hot, not boiling, water, stirring constantly, until the custard coats a metal spoon. Add vanilla and nutmeg to taste.

MINCEMEAT

1 lb.	chopped beef suet	500 g
3	large apples, peeled, cored and chopped	3
1½ lbs.	brown sugar	750 g
1½ lbs.	seeded raisins	750 g
1½ lbs.	currants	750 g
4 oz.	mixed lemon and orange peel	115 g
2	lemons, juice and grated rind	2
1 tsp.	cinnamon	5 mL
1 tsp.	nutmeg	5 mL
½ cup	brandy	125 mL

Mix all the ingredients very thoroughly in a large bowl. The brandy should be added gradually. Cover the mincemeat and leave it for a few days in a cool place, stirring it occasionally, then pack it in sterilized jars. Mincemeat should be made at least 3 weeks before you intend to use it. It will keep indefinitely in the refrigerator. Yields approximately 4 pints (2 L).

MINCE TARTS

5 cups	all-purpose flour	1.25 L
2 tsp.	salt	10 mL
2 tbsp.	brown sugar	30 mL
1 tsp.	baking powder	5 mL
1 lb.	shortening	454 g
1	egg	1
1 tbsp.	cider or malt vinegar	15 mL
	cold water	
	Mincemeat (see above)	
	pecan halves	

To make the pastry, mix the flour, salt, brown sugar and baking powder in a bowl. With a pastry blender, cut in the shortening until the mixture resembles coarse oatmeal. Beat the egg with the vinegar and add enough cold water to make 1 cup (250 mL) of liquid. Add the liquid to the dry mixture and mix with your hands, until the dough does not cling to the sides of the bowl. Shape the dough into a ball and wrap it in clear plastic. Refrigerate the dough until you are ready to use it. Roll out the pastry on a floured surface and cut it to fit the tart tins.

Line 16 to 20 tart tins with pastry and fill with prepared mincemeat. Garnish each tart with a pecan half. Bake for 20 minutes at 350°F (180°C). Serve the tarts warm.

4	eggs	4
2 cups	milk	500 mL
4 tbsp.	melted butter, cooled slightly	60 mL
1 tsp.	salt	5 mL
¼ tsp.	freshly grated nutmeg	1 mL
1 cup	all-purpose flour	250 mL
	soft butter for brushing the crêpe pan	
	Mincemeat, see recipe page 44	
⅓-½ cup	brandy or rum, warmed	75-125 mL
	vanilla ice cream	

Place the eggs, milk, butter, salt, nutmeg and flour in a bowl and thoroughly combine them with a wire whisk, until the mixture is smooth, or blend the ingredients in a blender or food processor. Refrigerate the batter for at least 2 hours. When you are ready to make the crêpes, heat a 6" or 7" (15-18 cm) crêpe pan and brush it lightly with butter. Drop 2 tablespoons (30 mL) of batter into the pan and rapidly tilt the pan to spread the batter evenly. Cook until the bottom is lightly browned, about 1 minute, turn the crêpe, and brown the other side.

Fill each crêpe with mincemeat, roll it up loosely, and place it in a buttered baking pan. Dot the tops with butter and heat in the oven at 350°F (180°C) for 15 to 20 minutes. Place the crêpes on a warm serving dish, pour the brandy or rum over them, and set the liquid aflame. Serve the crêpes with vanilla ice cream.

This recipe makes 24 crêpes, about 6" (15 cm) in diameter. Crêpes may be made in advance, stacked flat with waxed paper between them, and refrigerated or frozen. They should be thawed before filling and heating.

BREAKFAST OR BRUNCH

Serves 8

Broiled Grapefruit
Sautéed Veal Kidneys
Scrambled Eggs
Spicy Bran Muffins
Marmalade
Tea or Coffee

BROILED GRAPEFRUIT

4	large, top-quality, white or pink grapefruit	4
8 tbsp.	fruit sugar or honey	120 mL
8 tbsp.	sherry	120 mL

Cut each grapefruit in half. With a sharp knife, cut around each segment of fruit and remove any seeds. On each half, sprinkle approximately 1 tbsp. (15 mL) fruit sugar or honey. Place the grapefruit halves on a jelly roll pan or in a shallow baking dish and heat under the broiler 2-3" (5-7 cm) from the element. Remove from the oven, place on serving dishes, and sprinkle each half with 1 tbsp. (15 mL) sherry. Serve at once.

SAUTÉED VEAL KIDNEYS

4	veal kidneys	4
2-3 tbsps.	butter or bacon fat	30-45 mL
	salt and pepper to taste	
2 scant tbsp.	flour	scant 30 mL
1 cup	beef stock	250 mL
	lemon wedges or Worcestershire sauce	

Wash the kidneys and remove all the fat, skin and hard central membranes. Cut the kidneys into slices ½" (2.5 cm) thick. Melt the butter or bacon fat in a skillet, add the kidneys, season them with salt and pepper, and sauté them quickly until they are brown. Sprinkle the flour over the kidneys, blend it in thoroughly, slowly add the stock and mix. Simmer the mixture until the liquid is slightly thickened and smooth. Serve with lemon wedges or Worcestershire sauce.

SPICY BRAN MUFFINS

1 cup	All-Bran	250 mL
1 cup	milk	250 mL
1	egg	1
¼ cup	melted butter	50 mL
½ cup	seedless raisins or finely chopped pitted dates	125 mL
1 cup	sifted flour	250 mL
2½ tsp.	baking powder	12 mL
½ tsp.	salt	2 mL
¼ cup	sugar	50 mL
1 tsp.	cinnamon	5 mL
½ tsp.	nutmeg	2 mL

Combine the bran and milk, let stand until most of the moisture is absorbed, add egg and melted butter and beat well. Stir in raisins or dates. Sift together flour, baking powder, salt, sugar, cinnamon and nutmeg. Add to bran mixture, stirring only until combined. Fill greased muffin pans ⅔ full. Bake in a 400°F (200°C) oven for 20-25 minutes. Makes 12 muffins.

EASY ORANGE MARMALADE

5	medium marmalade oranges	5
2½ cups	water	625 mL
⅛ tsp.	baking soda	0.5 mL
6 cups	sugar	1.5 L
1	pouch liquid Certo	1

Using a very sharp knife, remove the peel from the oranges in 1½" (4 cm) wide strips. Remove as much white membrane as possible and cut the peel into fine slivers. Place the peel in a large pot, add the water and baking soda, and bring to a boil. Reduce heat and simmer, covered, for 20 minutes, stirring occasionally. Remove the white membrane from the oranges and section them, discarding the seeds. Add the fruit and its juice to the undrained cooked rind. Simmer, covered, for 10 minutes. Measure 3 cups (750 mL) of this mixture into a large saucepan. Add the sugar and mix well. Place over high heat and bring to a full rolling boil; boil hard for 1 minute, stirring constantly. Remove from heat and stir in the Certo. Skim off the foam with a metal spoon. Then, stir for approximately 7 minutes to cool the marmalade slightly and prevent floating fruit. Ladle the marmalade into glasses and cover each glass with paraffin. Makes 8 x 6-oz. (170 mL) glasses.

Serves 8

Curried Mushroom Soup
Cold Veal and Ham Pie
Red Cabbage and Celery Salad with Roquefort Dressing
Irish Coffee Jelly with Whipped Cream
Sugar Cookies
Molasses Cookies

CURRIED MUSHROOM SOUP

1½ tbsp.	butter	22 mL
¾ cup	finely diced mushrooms	175 mL
1½ tbsp.	flour	22 mL
	curry powder to taste	
4 cups	beef broth	1 L
¾ cup	heavy cream	175 mL
2	egg yolks, beaten	2
	whipped cream	

Heat the butter in a pan, add the mushrooms, and cook gently for about 5 minutes. Add the flour and curry powder and cook briefly, stirring with a whisk. Add the broth, stirring constantly. In a bowl, blend the cream and egg yolks. Remove the soup from the heat and add the yolk mixture to it, stirring constantly. Return the soup to the heat and cook until it is hot but not boiling. Pour the soup into hot cups, add a dollop of whipped cream to each cup, and serve immediately.

VEAL AND HAM PIE

2 lbs.	lean ham, cut in thin strips	1 kg
2 lbs.	lean boneless veal, cut in thin 1" squares	1 kg
2	onions, finely chopped	2
½ cup	finely chopped parsley	125 mL
1 tsp.	black pepper	5 mL
½ cup	chicken or beef broth	125 mL
1 tbsp.	Worcestershire sauce	15 mL
3 tbsp.	sherry	45 mL
	pastry for top (see recipe page 44 or use frozen puff pastry)	

On the bottom of a baking dish, place a layer of ham and cover it with a layer of veal. Sprinkle the meat with some of the chopped onion and parsley. Season with pepper, but no salt. Repeat the layers until all these ingredients are used up. Pour the broth over the meat and sprinkle with the Worcestershire sauce and sherry. Cover with pastry, make vents for steam to escape, and bake at 350°F (180°C) for 2 hours. Cool at room temperature for about an hour and then refrigerate.

RED CABBAGE AND CELERY SALAD

1	medium-sized red cabbage	1
1½ cups	finely chopped celery	375 mL
6	green onions, finely chopped	6

Remove the outer leaves and the core from the cabbage. Shred finely. Add the celery and onions. Allow a generous handful of salad mix per person. Combine lightly but thoroughly with approximately 1 cup (250 mL) of the Roquefort Dressing, recipe follows. Taste; chill until serving time.

ROQUEFORT DRESSING

1 tsp.	Dijon-style mustard	5 mL
½ tsp.	salt	2 mL
½ tsp.	pepper	2 mL
2-3 tbsp.	wine vinegar	30-45 mL
½ cup	olive oil	125 mL
¼ cup	heavy cream	50 mL
4-5 tbsp.	crumbled Roquefort cheese	60-75 mL

In a bowl, combine the mustard, salt and pepper. Whisk in the vinegar, oil then the cream. Add the cheese and continue to whisk until well-combined.

Irish Coffee Jelly

2 tbsp.	unflavoured gelatin (2 x 7 g env.)	30 mL
½ cup	cold water	125 mL
3 cups	hot strong coffee	750 mL
scant ½ cup	sugar	scant 125 mL
¾-1 cup	Irish whisky (if necessary, Scotch or Canadian will do)	175-250 mL
½ cup	whipped cream	125 mL
	chocolate sprinkles or coffee bean candy	

Dissolve the gelatin in the cold water. Pour the liquid into a bowl and add the coffee. Stir until the gelatin is thoroughly dissolved. (If necessary pour the liquid into a pan and heat it.) Add the sugar and stir. When the mixture has cooled, add the whisky, stir and pour the jelly into 8 demitasses. Refrigerate until the jelly is set. Before serving, top each cup with whipped cream and decorate with chocolate sprinkles or coffee bean candy. To serve, place each cup on its saucer with a coffee spoon.

Sugar Cookies

⅔ cup	butter	150 mL
⅔ cup	sugar	150 mL
2	eggs, beaten	2
1 tsp.	vanilla	5 mL
2 cups	sifted all-purpose flour	500 mL
1½ tsp.	baking powder	7 mL
½ tsp.	salt	2 mL

Cream the butter until it is fluffy. Add the sugar gradually. Add the eggs and vanilla. Add the flour, baking powder and salt, and mix thoroughly. Chill the dough for 2 hours or overnight. Roll it paper-thin on a floured board and cut it with fancy cookie cutters. Place the cookies on a greased cookie sheet, 2" (5 cm) apart, and bake in a preheated oven for about 5 minutes at 375°F (190°C). Makes 6 dozen cookies.

These cookies make a beautiful contrast to the traditional decorated sugar cookies. They are as effective on a Christmas tree as they are on a plate.

DOUGH

½ cup	butter	125 mL
¾ cup	sugar	175 mL
1	egg	1
¾ cup	molasses	175 mL
3½ cups	all-purpose flour	875 mL
¼ tsp.	salt	1 mL
1½ tsp.	cinnamon	7 mL
1½ tsp.	ginger	7 mL
1 tsp.	cloves	5 mL
1 tsp.	baking soda	5 mL
1 tsp.	grated lemon rind	5 mL

Cream butter and sugar, add egg and beat until light and fluffy. Add molasses and beat until blended. Stir in flour and other dry ingredients and grated lemon peel. Mix until well-blended. Refrigerate.

The following day, roll to ⅛" (3 mm) thickness, cut into fancy shapes with cutters and place 1" (2.5 cm) apart on greased cookie sheet. Bake 6 to 8 minutes in preheated 375°F (190°C) oven. Cool. Makes 8 to 9 dozen.

FROSTING

3¾ cups	icing sugar	900 mL
⅓ cup	egg whites	75 mL

Place the ingredients in a bowl and beat at medium speed until the mixture is smooth and stiff. Decorate cookies using the .3 or .4 small tip on pastry bag. This gives a clean thin white line of frosting. Store the cookies in a covered container.

As we prepare to cross the Channel from England to France, perhaps it is the moment to say a word in praise of wine — a subject on which the English and French have always been in complete agreement! Such an impeccable source of good advice as the Bible tells us "Drink no longer water, but use a little wine for thy stomach's sake" and also refers to "wine that maketh glad the heart of man". In a modest cookbook such as this, we would not presume to discuss the finer points of wine discrimination, about which learned volumes have been written. However, never have the joys of wine been so much appreciated by so many as today. Worldwide demand is putting some of the great vintages out of reach, but this should not discourage us unduly. "Vin ordinaire" from many countries is well worth sampling, and a glass of wine can turn a routine dinner into a festive occasion. Everyday cooking can also be enhanced by experimenting with wine to replace less flavourful liquids. Let us give the final word to Shakespeare: "Good wine is a good familiar creature if it be well used.".

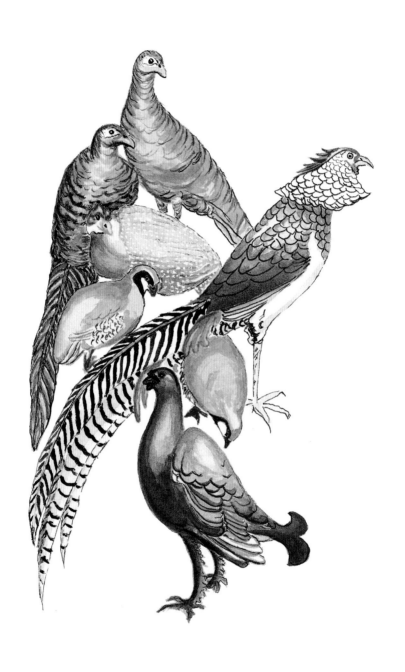

FRANCE

Drawing of a detail from a tapestry
"The First Sin"
woven in France, 20th Century.
Royal Ontario Museum
971.148
Gift of Mrs. Percyval Tudor-Hart.

FRANCE

In the beginning, the first irre- sistible temptation was connected with eating, and to many a foodlover, it would be Paradise
indeed if one were not constantly required to exercise restraint. An idyllic Eden
is charmingly pictured in a large modern French tapestry in the Textile Collections.
Eve has just taken a bite of the forbidden fruit and is offering it to Adam. The
lush garden surrounding them is alive with plants, flowers and creatures, and the
whole scene is bordered by a garland of mouth-watering fruits and vegetables.

It was in the magnificent setting of Versailles that Louis XIV, a prodigious eater,
made dining into a ceremony of elaborate ritual. His manners became the standard
of good taste, but it is interesting to note that he refused to use a fork, even
though the children of his household were being taught to master the "new utensil".
Knives and spoons had been used at table for a long time but solid food was held
in the fingers.

Forks first came to France from Italy in the 16th century, but their acceptance
must have been slow if Louis still declined their use a century later. Early forks
were two-tined, and at first they were employed more for serving than for eating.
By the late 17th century, however, forks were sufficiently popular to be included
in some of the travelling sets that fashionable gentlemen took on journeys. In the
European Department there is a case of cutlery containing a folding knife and
fork with cast silver handles, made in France in the late 17th century.

In 18th-century Europe the dinner services of the wealthy were magnificent, and
no piece lent itself so well to grandeur and fantasy as the soup tureen. Tureens
were made of silver, of porcelain, and of pottery, and they were originally ac-
companied by stands or platters. It became fashionable to mould tureens in unusual
shapes such as animal heads, ducks, turkeys, cabbages and artichokes. One can
imagine a steaming and delicious French potage being served from the European
Department's delightful turtle tureen.

TOWN AND COUNTRY

France was, and is, renowned for great elegance of interior furnishings and beauty and variety of countryside.

For a formal French dinner in town, use a cloth of toile or placemats of lace, set with sparkling crystal, delicate porcelain and silver. For a centrepiece, fill a crystal comport with grapes of two or three colours, decorated with shiny leaves and roses or carnations in water picks.

Most effective as a decoration for a country supper is a series of wine bottles marching down the centre of the table, with a single flower in each. Collect bottles of different shapes, sizes, and colours.

PICNIC OR COLD SUPPER

Serves 8

Crock of Chicken Liver Pâté with Melba Toast
Truite en Gelée with Herb Mayonnaise
or
Boiled Beef Tongue in Aspic
Mushroom Salad
with Mint Vinaigrette Dressing
Carrot and Zucchini Sticks
Fresh Fruit and Cheese

CHICKEN LIVER PÂTÉ

4	sprigs parsley	4
6 tbsp.	butter	90 mL
8 oz.	chicken livers	250 g
2 tbsp.	minced shallots or onions	30 mL
¼ cup	Madeira	50 mL
¼ cup	heavy cream	50 mL
⅛ tsp.	allspice	0.5 mL
	salt and pepper to taste	

In a food processor, chop the parsley finely. Melt 2 tbsp. (30 mL) butter in a skillet and sauté the livers in it for 2 to 3 minutes, until they are brown on the outside but still pink inside. Transfer them to the food processor. Sauté the shallots in the skillet until they are soft. Add the Madeira, stirring to loosen the brown bits in the pan, and simmer until the liquid is reduced by about half. Add the liquid to the food processor, together with the cream and seasonings, and purée until smooth. Add the remaining 4 tbsp. (60 mL) butter, melted and cooled slightly. Blend for 30 seconds. Pour the pâté into a crock, cover, and chill until firm.

MELBA TOAST

unsplit wiener rolls
butter

Slice the wiener rolls into rounds about ¼" (6 mm) thick. Butter the rounds lightly and place them on cookie sheets. Toast them in the oven at 250°F (120°C) for ½ hour, or until the rounds are lightly browned. Store leftover melba toast in an airtight cookie tin.

Truite En Gelée
With Herb Mayonnaise

8	trout, ¾-1 lb. (365-500 g) each, cleaned	8

COURT BOUILLON

	water to cover the fish	
1	medium onion, thinly sliced	1
1	bay leaf	1
½ tsp.	salt	2 mL
2	celery stalks with leaves	2
½ tsp.	thyme	2 mL
3	peppercorns	3
1 cup	dry white wine	250 mL

Place the fish in a single layer in a large baking pan. Add water to cover. Remove the fish and reserve. To the pan add remaining ingredients, except wine, and bring to a boil. Reduce heat and simmer about 5 minutes. Add wine and stir, then add the fish in a single layer. Poach gently for 10 to 12 minutes, or until the fish flakes but is still firm. Remove the trout from the pan and let cool. Reserve Court Bouillon. Remove heads, tails and skin and arrange trout on a platter. Refrigerate.

ASPIC

2 tbsp.	unflavoured gelatin (2 x 7 g pkgs.)	30 mL
½ cup	cold water	125 mL
3½ cups	Court Bouillon, hot, from previous recipe	875 mL
	parsley or dill	

Soften gelatin in cold water. Pour hot Court Bouillon into a saucepan. Add the softened gelatin and stir until it is dissolved. Remove saucepan from heat and chill liquid until it is on the point of setting. Coat trout with aspic (gently drizzle aspic over trout) and chill to set. Pour remaining aspic into a shallow dish; let set completely. Before serving, chop aspic and surround trout with it. Garnish with parsley or dill.

Herb Mayonnaise

1 cup	mayonnaise	250 mL
2 tsp.	finely chopped fresh dill	10 mL
2 tsp.	finely chopped fresh chives	10 mL
3 tbsp.	finely chopped watercress leaves	45 mL
1-2 tbsp.	fresh lemon juice	15-30 mL
½ tsp.	grated lemon rind	2 mL

Blend all ingredients in a bowl. Cover and chill for 1 to 2 hours.

Boiled Beef Tongue In Aspic

1	beef tongue, preferably pickled	1
1	medium onion, sliced	1
2-3	celery stalks with leaves	2-3
1-2	carrots, sliced	1-2
2	bay leaves	2
6-8	peppercorns	6-8
	stuffed olives	

Put the tongue in a pot and add all other ingredients, except olives. Just cover with boiling water. Simmer until the tongue is tender, about 3 hours. Leave the tongue in the pot until it is lukewarm. Remove tongue from the pot and take off the skin and the roots. Chill. Cut in ¼" (6 mm), or thinner, slices. Arrange overlapping slices of tongue, in rows, in a shallow serving dish, with a row of stuffed olives in the centre.

ASPIC

2 tbsp.	unflavoured gelatin (2 x 7 g pkgs.)	30 mL
½ cup	cold water	125 mL
2 x 10 oz.	cans condensed beef bouillon	2 x 284 mL
1 cup	white wine	250 mL

Soften gelatin in the water. In a saucepan bring 1 can of bouillon to a boil and add gelatin, stirring until it is dissolved. Stir in remaining bouillon and wine. Chill aspic until it is slightly set. Pour over tongue and chill until aspic is firm.

Mushroom Salad

1 lb.	fresh mushrooms, thinly sliced	500 g
½ cup	very thinly sliced celery	125 mL
¼-½ cup	very thinly sliced water chestnuts	50-125 mL

Put all ingredients in a serving bowl. Cover and leave in a cool place until you are ready to serve. Toss with Mint Vinaigrette Dressing, below, before serving.

Mint Vinaigrette Dressing

1 cup	olive oil	250 mL
4 tbsp.	mint vinegar, see page 169, or wine vinegar	60 mL
1-2 tbsp.	finely chopped fresh mint	15-30 mL
4 tsp.	Dijon-style mustard	20 mL
¼ tsp.	sugar	1 mL
¼ tsp.	salt	1 mL
	freshly ground pepper	

Blend all ingredients with a wire whisk, blender or food processor.

Serves 8

Onion Tart
or
Crêpes with Spinach and Chicken Filling
or
Sweetbreads and Ham Filling
and Sherry Cheese Sauce
or
Oxtail Soup
Salad of Assorted Greens
Walnut Oil Dressing
Baguette
Raspberry Mousseline

ONION TART

pastry recipe, see page 44

Make 2, 9" (23 cm) pie shells and freeze the remainder. Bake pie shells in 400°F (200°C) oven for 10 to 12 minutes, being careful not to brown too much.

FILLING

2 tbsp.	vegetable oil	30 mL
6 tbsp.	butter	90 mL
4 lbs.	onions, diced	2 kg
3½ tbsp.	flour	52 mL
6	eggs	6
2 cups	light cream	500 mL
2 tsp.	salt	10 mL
¼ tsp.	pepper	1 mL
⅛ tsp.	nutmeg	0.5 mL
⅛ tsp.	cayenne pepper	0.5 mL
2 cups	grated Swiss cheese	500 mL
2 tbsp.	butter	30 mL

In a heavy pan, heat the oil and 6 tbsp. (90 mL) butter. Add the onions and cook over low heat, until they are very tender and transparent, stirring occasionally. Sprinkle the onions with the flour and continue to cook for 2-3 minutes. Cool slightly. Pour half the onion mixture into each of the 2 pie shells. Beat the eggs, cream and seasonings until they are well-blended. Mix in half the cheese. Pour half the mixture over the onions in each pie shell and sprinkle with the remaining cheese. Dot the tops with butter. Bake in the upper third of the oven, preheated to 375°F (190°C) for 25 to 30 minutes, or until the tarts are puffed and browned.

CRÊPES

See recipe, page 45, makes 16 crêpes.

SPINACH AND CHICKEN FILLING

2 tbsp.	butter	30 mL
½ lb.	mushrooms, finely chopped	250 g
1	large onion, finely chopped	1
1 lb.	fresh spinach or 10 oz. (283 g) pkg. frozen, cooked, well-drained, and finely chopped	500 g
2 cups	diced cooked chicken	500 mL
¼ cup	sour cream	50 mL
2 tbsp.	dry sherry	30 mL
½ tsp.	salt	2 mL
⅛ tsp.	cayenne pepper	0.5 mL
¼ tsp.	ground nutmeg	1 mL

Melt the butter in a heavy skillet, add the mushrooms and onion, and sauté them until they are soft. If the mushrooms create a great deal of liquid, raise the heat for a minute to evaporate the excess. Add the spinach, chicken, sour cream, sherry and seasonings, and stir.

Put 1 tbsp. (15-30mL) of filling on each crêpe and roll it up. Arrange the crêpes in a single layer, fold-side down, in a shallow, buttered baking dish. Pour the Sherry Cheese Sauce, page 62, over them and bake at 350°F (180°C) until the sauce is bubbling and lightly browned — about 30-45 minutes.

The filling is sufficient for 16 crêpes. The filled crêpes may be frozen, but allow 2 hours for defrosting.

1½-2 lbs.	sweetbreads, cooked and cubed	750 g-1 kg
	boiling water	
2 tbsp.	lemon juice	30 mL
1	small onion, chopped	1
2	celery stalks and leaves or 3-4 parsley sprigs, chopped	2
4 tbsp.	butter	60 mL
½ lb.	boiled ham, cubed	250 g
1	green pepper, diced	1
½ lb.	mushrooms, sliced	250 g
½ cup	dry sherry	125 mL
1 cup	heavy cream	250 mL
½ tsp.	salt	2 mL
	freshly ground pepper to taste	

To prepare the sweetbreads, drop them into boiling water containing lemon juice, chopped onion and celery or parsley. The water should cover the sweetbreads. Lower the heat and simmer for 20 minutes. Drain the sweetbreads, plunge them immediately into cold water and leave for 15 minutes. Drain again, remove the skin and membrane, and cut in cubes.

In a skillet, melt the butter, add sweetbreads, ham and green pepper, sauté for 10 minutes, stirring frequently. Add mushrooms and cook for 5 minutes. Do not let the mixture come to a boil. The filling is sufficient for 16 crêpes.

Fill, top with Sherry Cheese Sauce, recipe follows, and bake crêpes according to instructions in the preceding recipe.

SHERRY CHEESE SAUCE

4 tbsp.	butter	60 mL
4 tbsp.	flour	60 mL
1½ cups	chicken stock	375 mL
1 cup	milk	250 mL
½ cup	grated Parmesan cheese	125 mL
½ cup	grated Swiss cheese	125 mL
½ cup	dry sherry	125 mL
	cayenne pepper to taste	
	salt to taste	

In a large saucepan, melt the butter, stir in flour, and cook gently for 1-2 minutes. Slowly blend in the combined chicken stock and milk and cook over low heat, stirring constantly, until the sauce is smooth and thickened. Add the cheeses, sherry, cayenne and salt. Stir until the cheese is melted. Makes 3½ cups (875 mL) of sauce.

1 tbsp.	butter	15 mL
1 tbsp.	vegetable oil	15 mL
3-4 lbs.	oxtail, cut in 1" (2.5 cm) sections	1.5-2 kg
1	onion, sliced	1
3	carrots, sliced	3
1	celery stalk, sliced	1
2 tbsp.	flour	30 mL
2 qts.	beef stock	2 L
	bouquet garni, instructions follow	
½ tsp.	thyme	2 mL
5	peppercorns	5
⅔ cup	finely diced carrots	150 mL
⅔ cup	finely diced celery	150 mL
⅔ cup	finely diced turnips	150 mL
	salt and pepper	
3 tbsp.	Madeira	45 mL

In a deep frying pan or heavy pot, gently heat the butter and oil. Add the oxtail pieces and cook until they are golden brown on all sides. Transfer the meat to a plate. To the pot, add the sliced onion, carrot and celery, and cook until they are soft and lightly browned. Add the flour and continue to cook until it is brown, stirring constantly. Remove the pot from the heat and allow the mixture to cool a little. Gradually, stir in the beef stock and return the pot to the stove. Bring the mixture to a boil and cook until it is smooth and slightly thickened, stirring frequently. Return the oxtail to the pot, add the bouquet garni, thyme and peppercorns, and bring to a boil over high heat. Skim the fat off the surface, reduce the heat, and simmer, covered, for 3½ hours. Remove the oxtail and strain the liquid into a large bowl. After it settles, skim off the fat again. Discard the bones from the oxtails and return the meat and the liquid to the pot, add the diced carrot, celery and turnip, and simmer for 30 minutes. Season to taste with salt and pepper. Stir in the Madeira and serve.

Bouquet Garni

3	sprigs fresh parsley	3
3	sprigs fresh thyme, or ¼ tsp. (1 mL) dried	3
1	bay leaf	1

Tie all the ingredients in a cheesecloth bag.

SALAD OF ASSORTED GREENS

See recipe, page 16.
Dress salad with Walnut Oil Dressing, recipe follows.

WALNUT OIL DRESSING

¼ cup	wine vinegar	50 mL
1 tbsp.	Dijon-style mustard	15 mL
¾ cup	walnut oil	175 mL
	salt and pepper	

Beat together the vinegar and mustard. Add the oil in a stream, beating until the dressing is well blended. Add salt and pepper to taste. Makes about 1 cup (250 mL).

RASPBERRY MOUSSELINE

2 x 12-oz.	pkgs. frozen raspberries	2 x 340 g
½ cup	sugar	125 mL
1 tbsp.	lemon juice	15 mL
2 tbsp.	unflavoured gelatin (2 x 7 g pkgs.)	30 mL
½ cup	cold water	125 mL
1 tsp.	vanilla	5 mL
1 cup	heavy cream, whipped	250 mL
	sprigs of mint	

Defrost the raspberries and strain the juice into a saucepan. Add the sugar and heat until it is dissolved. Add the lemon juice. Soften the gelatin in the cold water and add it to the hot mixture, stirring until the gelatin is dissolved. Add the vanilla and stir. Chill until the mixture begins to thicken. Fold in the whipped cream and half the berries. Rinse a 1½-quart (1.5 L) mould in cold water, dry it and pour the raspberry mixture into it. Chill overnight. To serve, unmould the mousseline onto a serving plate and garnish it with the remaining berries and a few sprigs of mint.

Frozen strawberries may be substituted for raspberries.

DINNER

Serves 8

Mushroom Consommé
Parmesan Toasts
Broiled Sole
Baked Tomatoes with Thyme
Boiled Potatoes
Pears in Red Wine
Pistachio Cookies

MUSHROOM CONSOMMÉ

2 tbsp.	butter	30 mL
¼ lb.	fresh mushrooms, finely chopped	125 g
2-3	green onions, finely chopped	2-3
1 tbsp.	flour	15 mL
3 tbsp.	finely chopped parsley	45 mL
6 cups	beef or chicken stock	1.5 L
	salt and pepper to taste	
½ cup	heavy cream, whipped	125 mL
	nutmeg	

In a large saucepan, melt the butter and sauté the mushrooms and onion in it for about 5 minutes. Add the flour, stirring until it is well blended. Then add the parsley, stock, salt and pepper, and mix and heat. Serve the soup in heated cups, garnished with a dollop of whipped cream and a dash of nutmeg.

PARMESAN TOASTS

1	baguette or Italian loaf	1
1 cup	mayonnaise	250 mL
½-¾ cup	freshly grated Parmesan cheese	125-175 mL
1	green onion, finely chopped	1

Cut bread into rounds or squares ¼" (6 mm) thick. Mix mayonnaise, cheese and onion together until well combined. Spread generously on bread, place on a baking sheet and toast, under the broiler, until delicately browned, or bake in a 350°F (180°C) oven.

Serve hot with drinks or soup.

BROILED SOLE

½ cup	melted butter	125 mL
2 tbsp.	lemon juice	30 mL
1 tsp.	mayonnaise	5 mL
¼ tsp.	paprika	1 mL
5 lbs.	sole fillets	2.2 kg
1 cup	chopped parsley	250 mL
½ cup	melted butter	125 mL
2	lemons, cut into 8 wedges each	2

To make basting sauce, melt butter and whisk in lemon juice, mayonnaise and paprika. Preheat broiler. Arrange fillets, skin side down, on a greased broiling pan. Brush with basting sauce. Broil 3" (7 cm) from heat 3 to 4 minutes (until easily flaked). Baste fillets with the sauce once during cooking. When they are done, remove to a heated serving platter, sprinkle with parsley and keep warm.

To the remainder of the basting sauce, add the other ½ cup (125 mL) butter and heat to the boiling point. Pour over parsleyed fillets. Garnish with lemon wedges.

BAKED TOMATOES WITH THYME

8	medium tomatoes	8
½ cup	sugar	125 mL
	thyme	
	salt and pepper	
2½ cups	soft bread crumbs	600 mL
⅓ cup	melted butter	75 mL

Peel and core tomatoes and place in a shallow baking dish. Sprinkle with sugar, thyme, salt and pepper. Fill in around the tomatoes with 1¼ cups (300 mL) of the bread crumbs. Add the remaining 1¼ cups (300 mL) bread crumbs to the melted butter and sprinkle over the tomatoes. Bake in a 350°F (180°C) oven for about 45 minutes.

PEARS IN RED WINE

1½ cups	red wine	375 mL
1½ cups	water	375 mL
1 cup	sugar	250 mL
1	stick cinnamon	1
3 x 1½"	strips lemon rind	3 x 4 cm
8	pears, all the same size	8
2½ tbsp.	cornstarch	37 mL

Put the wine and water into a large saucepan and add the sugar, cinnamon and lemon rind. Cook over low heat until the sugar is dissolved, stirring constantly. Peel the pears and place them in the saucepan. They should be almost covered by the syrup. Simmer for 10-20 minutes, depending on the ripeness of the pears. Lift the pears out of the saucepan and arrange them on a serving dish. Blend the cornstarch with a few spoonfuls of the syrup from the pan. Add the cornstarch mixture to the syrup in the saucepan and simmer for 2 minutes. Strain the syrup over the pears and chill for several hours before serving. The pears may be served with whipped cream or sour cream flavoured with cinnamon.

PISTACHIO COOKIES

⅔ cup	butter	150 mL
1 cup	sugar	250 mL
1	egg	1
1 tsp.	vanilla	5 mL
½ tsp.	almond extract	2 mL
2 cups	all-purpose flour	500 mL
1½ tsp.	baking powder	7 mL
½ tsp.	salt	2 mL
	food colouring	
6 oz.	semisweet chocolate, melted over hot water	170 g
1 cup	finely chopped pistachio nuts	250 mL

In a bowl, beat the butter, sugar, egg, vanilla and almond extract until the mixture is light and fluffy. Sift in the flour, baking powder and salt, and beat until the ingredients are combined. Measure out ¾ cup (175 mL) of dough and put it in a separate bowl. Add food colouring (a pale green is very attractive) and ¼ cup (50 mL) nuts to the first part and stir. Form the coloured dough into a roll about 10" (25 cm) long and 1¼" (3 cm) in diameter and wrap it in waxed paper. Form the remaining dough into a rectangle 10" by 4¼" (25 x 10 cm) and wrap it in waxed paper. Refrigerate both packages of dough for 1 hour. Place the roll in the centre of the rectangle. Carefully mould the rectangle around the roll, until the coloured dough is completely encircled. Wrap in waxed paper and refrigerate overnight.

With a sharp knife, cut the roll of dough into slices ⅛" (3 mm) thick. Place the slices on a lightly greased cookie sheet, 2" (5 cm) apart. Bake in a preheated oven at 375°F (190°C) for 8-10 minutes. Remove the cookies from the cookie sheet and allow them to cool. Dip the cookies in the melted chocolate and then in the remaining nuts. Refrigerate the cookies until the chocolate is firmly set and then store them in a covered container. Makes 6 dozen cookies.

Pecans or walnuts may be used instead of pistachios, if you prefer their flavour.

DINNER

Serves 8

Snails in Mushroom Caps
Veal Suprême
Green Beans
Braised Celeriac
Boston or Iceberg Lettuce Salad
with Lemon Chive Dressing
Chocolate Hazelnut Pots de Crème

SNAILS IN MUSHROOM CAPS

24	mushrooms, large enough to hold a snail	24
24	snails	24
	snail butter, recipe follows	

Remove the stems and clean the mushroom caps with a damp cloth. In each cap place a snail and then pack the cavity with Snail Butter. Put the mushrooms in a shallow casserole and bake in a preheated oven at 400°F (200°C) for 10 minutes, or until the mushrooms are tender and the butter bubbly.

SNAIL BUTTER

1 cup	butter, softened	250 mL
4 tbsp.	finely minced shallots, scallions, or onion	60 mL
2-4	garlic cloves, mashed, or garlic to taste	2-4
4 tbsp.	minced parsley	60 mL
	salt and pepper to taste	

Thoroughly combine all the ingredients in a bowl. It is difficult to judge the correct amount of butter required, because snails and mushrooms vary in size. Leftover snail butter may be used on vegetables or to make garlic bread.

BOSTON OR ICEBERG LETTUCE SALAD

2	heads Boston or iceberg lettuce	2
	parsley or watercress sprigs	
	Lemon Chive Dressing, page 16	

Cut the heads of lettuce in wedges, or slice them crosswise. Arrange the wedges or slices on individual salad plates and garnish with sprigs of parsley or watercress. Serve the Lemon Chive Dressing in a separate bowl.

VEAL SUPRÊME

2 tbsp.	butter	30 mL
2 tbsp.	vegetable oil	30 mL
4 lbs.	veal	2 kg
¼ cup	butter	50 mL
2	onions, sliced	2
2	carrots, sliced	2
	Duxelles, recipe follows	
	Velouté Sauce, recipe follows	
½ cup	grated Gruyère cheese	125 mL

This dish may be made with top round, boned loin, or filets of veal. If you use top round or loin, have the butcher try to produce a roast of cylindrical shape about 4" (10 cm) in diameter. If you use filets, you will require 4.

In a large skillet, heat the 2 tbsp. (30 mL) of butter and the oil and brown the veal in it, being careful not to burn the butter. Remove the meat from the skillet, rub it with the ¼ cup (50 mL) of butter, and set it in a roasting pan. To the skillet, add the onions and carrots and cook them for 5 minutes, but do not brown them. Add the vegetables to the roasting pan. Bake, covered, for 1½-2 hours or until a meat thermometer registers 175°F (80°C), basting the roast every 20 minutes or so with the butter in the pan. If you use filets, check them when they have been in the oven 1 hour. Since they are smaller, they will cook faster. The veal is cooked if the juices run clear when the meat is pricked with a fork. Remove the meat from the pan and let it stand for 30 minutes before slicing.

Strain roasting pan juices into a saucepan and skim off fat. Boil juices until reduced to 1 cup (250 mL). Use this cup of liquid for the Velouté Sauce.

Cut the roast into slices ½" (1.3 cm) thick. Spread each slice with a layer of Duxelles. Reassemble the roast by putting the slices together again in the original shape. Put the roast in a baking dish and cover it loosely with aluminum foil. Heat at 350°F (180°C) for 20 to 30 minutes, check after 20 minutes.

Remove roast from oven and pour hot Velouté Sauce over it. Sprinkle with cheese and broil for 4-5 minutes; or until lightly browned. Serve immediately.

The meat may be prepared in advance up to the point of reheating, as may the Velouté Sauce. Warm sauce in a double boiler over very low heat.

DUXELLES

4 tbsp.	butter	60 mL
2	onions, finely chopped	2
1½ lbs.	mushrooms, finely chopped, pat dry	750 g
	salt and pepper to taste	

In a skillet, melt butter and sauté onions until soft. Add mushrooms; cook over high heat for 5-6 minutes. Remove from heat; season with salt and pepper.

VELOUTÉ SAUCE

2 tbsp.	butter	30 mL
2 tbsp.	flour	30 mL
1 cup	reduced pan juices from veal roast	250 mL
1 cup	hot milk	250 mL
	salt and pepper to taste	
	few grains nutmeg	
½ cup	grated Gruyère cheese	125 mL

In a saucepan, melt the butter and add the flour to it. Cook, stirring constantly, until the mixture is bubbly. Add the hot reduced pan juices and milk and beat with a wire whisk. Cook until the sauce is thickened. Season with salt, pepper and nutmeg. Remove from heat and stir in the cheese.

BRAISED CELERIAC

2	large celery roots	2
2	onions, chopped	2
2 tbsp.	butter	30 mL
2 cups	beef broth	500 mL
	salt and pepper	

Pare celery roots and cut in ¼" (6 mm) slices. Sauté onions in butter until limp. Place a layer of half the celery root slices in a shallow casserole. Cover with onions and another layer of celery root. Pour in stock to just cover vegetables. Cover loosely with foil. Cook in a 350°F (180°C) oven for 1 hour, basting occasionally. Toward the end of the cooking time, remove foil and let liquid be absorbed. Season if necessary.

CHOCOLATE HAZELNUT POTS DE CRÈME

½ cup	shelled hazelnuts	125 mL
6 oz.	semisweet chocolate bits	170 g
1 oz.	unsweetened chocolate, cut in small pieces	30 g
1 cup	light cream	250 mL
4 tbsp.	milk	60 mL
4	egg yolks	4
	pinch of salt	

In a food processor or a blender, reduce the hazelnuts to a powder. Loosen the powder thoroughly from the sides with a rubber spatula. Add the semisweet chocolate bits and the unsweetened chocolate. Heat the cream and milk together, do not boil, and pour the liquid into the blender or processor. Blend on high or process briefly until the mixture is smooth. Add the egg yolks and salt and blend again. Pour the crème into pots de crème cups or champagne glasses. Chill in the refrigerator and remove 1 hour before serving. Serves 4, repeat recipe for 8.

ITALY

Drawing of "Faustina Bel" plate,
Majolica, Italy, 16th century.
Royal Ontario Museum
915. 5. 126
Gift of Sir Edmund Osler

ITALY

The dinner party was the main feature of social life in ancient Rome. The houses of the well- to-do always had a formal dining room, called the triclinium, and there was often a dining table in the enclosed central courtyard as well. Usually three couches were arranged in a U-shape around the table, each one large enough to accommodate three reclining guests. An intimate dinner was planned for three to nine people — "not less than the Graces nor more than the Muses".

In the Roman Gallery is a collection of bronze cooking vessels found in the ruins of a Roman house in Egypt. Who today would not prefer the strainer with lotus flowers decorating its handle and a bird's head hook, to the plastic model hidden under the sink? It was made in the late second or first century B.C.

By the 1st century A.D., the Roman housewife of moderate means was able to afford fine tableware that was produced in Gaul and traded all over the Roman world. This pottery, known as Samian ware, has a warm, glossy orange-red surface. Both plain and skillfully decorated pieces were available. Plain forms were made on the potter's wheel and then dipped in a liquid slip before firing. Those with characteristic relief decoration were produced in moulds. Motifs included mythological and human figures, birds, plants and ornamental patterns, reminiscent of decoration on earlier metal vessels. Samian pieces were produced in standard sizes, so that purchasers could replace broken dishes with new ones of the right size — much in the manner of open-stock tableware today. The elegant pieces of Samian ware were kept to grace the dining table, and the coarser examples would have been used in the kitchen for cooking or storage.

A great contrast to the classical ware is provided by the vibrantly coloured Italian majolica plates in the European Department. Tin-glazed earthenware was first made in the Near East and was introduced into Spain by the Islamic conquerors. The name "majolica" derives from the island of Majorca, from where the Spanish wares were first imported into Italy. The ware is called faïence in France, Delft in Holland, and delftware in England.

Eminent Italian artists painted majolica plates, notably the Calamelli family, active in Faenza; the Andreoli family active at Gubbio; and Nicola Pellipario, active at Casteldurante and Urbino. Their magnificent motifs included historical, mythological, and religious scenes; views of daily life, and portraits. The examples of "Ipolita Bella" and "Faustina Bella" majolica plates in the Museum collections would have been made specifically as betrothal gifts for the brides depicted on them.

A ROMAN FEAST

Italy is a land of sunny skies, brilliantly coloured flowers in a warm terracotta background, green pines, and cascading water in omnipresent fountains.

For a centrepiece that evokes a fountain, use an alabaster tiered comport, or make a tiered receptacle of plates and goblets to achieve the same effect. Fill it with pine branches and carnations. Or use a basket overflowing with artichokes, green peas and fresh figs; tomatoes, mushrooms, peppers and parsley would be equally attractive. Whatever you choose as your centrepiece, your table mats should be of a bright clear colour to accent it. Brightly striped napkins would make the perfect finishing touch.

Serves 8

Antipasto
Fettuccine
with Julienne of Ham or Chicken
Pears and Gorgonzola Cheese
or
Fresh Strawberries
with Zabaglione

ANTIPASTO

What you serve depends on your imagination or what special foods are in season. Your choices may be arranged on platters or shallow serving dishes and garnished to please your eye. Thinly sliced and buttered light or dark rye bread should accompany the antipasto. The following are simply a few suggestions for ingredients: green and black olives, marinated mushrooms, marinated artichokes, tuna, sardines, sliced ham, salami, hard-cooked eggs.

An attractive antipasto platter might begin with a can of solid white tuna, drained and set in the centre of the platter. Arrange other choices in a wheel around the tuna. Eggs should be halved or quartered. Ham looks appealing in slender rolls. Marinated artichoke hearts may be purchased, or you may use canned artichoke hearts and marinate them for several hours in Lemon Chive Dressing, see recipe page 16. The recipe that follows yields very tasty marinated mushrooms.

Marinated Mushrooms

¾ cup	olive oil	175 mL
½ cup	water	125 mL
2	lemons, juice of	2
1	large garlic clove, peeled and halved	1
6-8	peppercorns	6-8
½ tsp.	salt	2 mL
1 lb.	fresh button mushrooms	500 g
4 tbsp.	finely chopped fresh dill	60 mL

Combine all the ingredients, except the mushrooms and dill, in an enamelled or stainless steel saucepan, and bring to a boil. Reduce heat, cover, and simmer for 15 minutes. Strain the marinade and return it to the saucepan. Add the mushrooms and simmer for 5 minutes, stirring occasionally. Remove from heat and allow to cool. Pour the mixture into a bowl, cover, and refrigerate until you are ready to serve. Remove the mushrooms from the marinade, arrange them on the platter, and sprinkle them with dill.

Fettuccine With Julienne Ham Or Chicken

1½ lbs.	fresh fettuccine	750 g
1 cup	heavy cream	250 mL
¼ lb.	soft butter	125 g
2 cups	freshly grated, imported Parmesan cheese	500 mL
1½-2 cups	julienne of cooked ham or chicken at room temperature	375-500 mL
	salt and freshly ground black pepper	

Cook the fettuccine in 5 quarts (5 L) of rapidly boiling water for 2-5 minutes. If you use packaged noodles, cook according to directions on the package. Drain the noodles in a colander. Heat the cream and butter in the fettuccine pan and return the fettuccine to the pan to reheat. Gradually add 1 cup (250 mL) of the cheese, tossing the fettuccine to coat. Add the ham or chicken and mix gently. Season to taste with salt and pepper. Serve in a heated bowl. Serve the extra cheese in a separate bowl.

—Fresh Strawberries With Zabaglione—

3 pints	strawberries, washed and hulled	1.5 L
	zabaglione (recipe follows)	

Arrange the strawberries in an attractive bowl and serve with Zabaglione.

Zabaglione

8	egg yolks	8
1 cup	sugar	250 mL
½ tsp.	salt	2 mL
½-¾ cup	Marsala*	125-175 mL
½ cup	heavy cream, whipped	125 mL

Bring water in the bottom of a double boiler to a simmer (not a full boil). Put the egg yolks, sugar, salt and Marsala in the top. Heat until the mixture is thickened, beating constantly with an electric mixer or rotary beater. Scrape the sides and bottom of the pot occasionally. Pour the mixture into a bowl and chill it in the refrigerator. When the mixture is thoroughly chilled, fold in the whipped cream. Transfer to a serving bowl.

* Sweet sherry, Madeira, or port may be used instead of Marsala.

Serves 8

Fisherman's Stew with Crusty Bread
or
Spinach Soufflé Ring and
Creamed Ham and Eggs
with Hot Buttered Toast

Salad of Assorted Greens
with Walnut Oil Dressing

Whole Oranges Suprême

FISHERMAN'S STEW

¼ cup	olive oil	50 mL
1 cup	finely chopped onion	250 mL
1 tbsp.	finely minced garlic	15 mL
1½ cups	dry white wine	375 mL
4 tbsp.	tomato paste	60 mL
2 cups	water	500 mL
1½ cups	bottled clam juice	375 mL
2	bay leaves	2
⅛ tsp.	thyme	0.5 mL
½ tsp.	ground fennel	2 mL
	salt	
8	small frozen lobster tails	8
1 lb.	each of 2 kinds of firm white fish	500 g
1 lb.	scallops	500 g
4 tbsp.	chopped parsley	60 mL
1	lemon, grated rind of	1

Heat the oil in a large saucepan and sauté the onions in it for 5 minutes. Add the garlic and cook for a minute longer. Add the wine and boil briskly for a few minutes. Stir the tomato paste into the water, add to onion mixture with clam juice and herbs. Salt to taste carefully since clam juice can be salty. Reduce the heat and simmer, partly covered, for 10 minutes. This sauce may be made in advance and refrigerated.

Thaw lobster tails. Cut shells almost to the end of the tail with strong shears, or cut along the underside with scissors. Cut the white fish into bite-sized pieces.

At serving time, bring sauce to a boil, drop in lobster tails and fish. Reduce heat; simmer for 5 minutes. Add scallops; simmer 5 minutes more. Divide seafood among 8 soup plates, spoon sauce over and sprinkle with parsley and lemon rind.

Fisherman's stew is flexible. Shrimps, clams, or mussels may be used in place of lobster. Add each ingredient to the sauce only for as long as is required for cooking.

Spinach Soufflé Ring

4 tbsp.	butter	60 mL
6 tbsp.	flour	90 mL
2 cups	milk	500 mL
6	eggs, separated	6
2 tsp.	salt	10 mL
¼ tsp.	pepper	1 mL
2 cups	cooked spinach, well-drained and finely chopped	500 mL
¼ cup	finely chopped onion	50 mL

In a large saucepan, melt the butter. Stir in the flour and cook gently for 1-2 minutes. Add the milk gradually and cook slowly until the sauce has thickened. Cool the sauce slightly. Beat the egg yolks with the salt and pepper and add them to the cream sauce. Add the spinach and onion and stir until well-mixed. Beat the egg whites until stiff and fold them into the spinach mixture. Pour into a greased 7-cup (1.75 L) ring mould. Set the mould in a pan of hot water and bake at 350°F (180°C) for 55 minutes. Let the soufflé stand for 10 minutes before unmoulding onto a heated platter.

Creamed Ham And Eggs

6 tbsp.	butter	90 mL
6 tbsp.	flour	90 mL
3 cups	hot milk	750 mL
2 tsp.	salt	10 mL
½ tsp.	pepper	2 mL
1½ cups	grated Asiago cheese	375 mL
8	hard-cooked eggs, quartered	8
3 cups	cooked ham, in small cubes	750 mL

In a saucepan, melt the butter. Stir in the flour and cook gently for 1-2 minutes. Add the milk gradually and cook slowly until the sauce has thickened, stirring constantly. Season with the salt and pepper. Add the cheese and stir until it is melted and well combined. Add the eggs and ham and heat well.

Fill centre of spinach ring with ham mixture; serve the remainder separately.

Salad Of Assorted Greens

See recipe, page 16.

Walnut Oil Dressing

See recipe, page 64.

8	large navel oranges	8
2 cups	cold water	500 mL
1¼ cups	sugar	300 mL
1½ cups	light corn syrup	375 mL
1½ cups	cold water	375 mL
¼ cup	lemon juice	50 mL
¼ cup	honey	50 mL
¼ cup	Cointreau	50 mL
	red food colouring	
	angelica or candied violets	

With a sharp knife, remove the rind from 4 oranges in 1½" (4 cm) wide strips. Remove as much white membrane as possible from the rind and cut into fine slivers. Peel the remaining oranges, remove the membrane from all 8, and place them in a large, fairly shallow bowl.

In a saucepan, combine the slivered peel and the 2 cups (500 mL) of cold water. Cover and bring to a boil. Remove from heat, drain, and reserve the rind. In a large saucepan, combine the sugar and corn syrup with 1½ cups (375 mL) of cold water and heat, stirring until the sugar is dissolved. Continue to cook, uncovered, over medium heat for 10 minutes. Add the reserved rind. Continue cooking for about 30 minutes, or until the mixture is slightly thickened. Remove from heat and stir in the lemon juice, honey, Cointreau and food colouring (whatever amount that gives a result that pleases you). Pour the hot syrup over the oranges. Cover and refrigerate for at least 8 hours, turning the oranges occasionally.

Remove the chilled oranges from the refrigerator at least ½ hour before serving. Decorate with strips of angelica or candied violets to delight your guests. The leftover syrup may be refrigerated and used to flavour and sweeten fruit compote.

DINNER

Serves 8

Prosciutto and Melon
Veal Marsala
Artichokes and Mushrooms
Cherry Tomatoes
Cream Cheese Dessert with Berry Sauce
or
Cassata alla Siciliana
or
Bisque Tortoni

PROSCIUTTO AND MELON

1	large or 2 small melons*	1 or 2
¾ lb.	prosciutto, sliced paper thin	365 g
	watercress or parsley	

Cut the melon into crescent-shaped slices about 1" (2.5 cm) wide at the centre. Peel and remove the pulp and seeds. Arrange 3 slices on each of 8 plates, along with 2 or 3 slices of prosciutto. Garnish with watercress or parsley.

*Cantaloupe, cassaba, honeydew, etc.

3 lbs.	veal scallops, pounded to ¼" (6 mm) thickness	1.5 kg
	flour	
2 tbsp.	butter, or more if required	30 mL
3 tbsp.	olive oil	45 mL
	salt and pepper	
1 cup	Marsala wine	250 mL
1 cup	chicken or beef stock	250 mL
2 tbsp.	soft butter	30 mL

Dip the veal scallops in flour and shake them to remove excess flour. In a heavy pan, gently heat 2 tbsp. (30 mL) butter and the olive oil. Add the veal scallops and brown them on both sides. Transfer them to a heated plate and season with salt and pepper to taste.

Pour off the fat from pan, add the Marsala and ½ cup (125 mL) stock, and boil for about 1 minute. Return the veal scallops to the pan to heat them. Transfer them to a serving platter and keep them warm in the oven while you prepare a sauce from the liquid in the pan.

To the pan, add the rest of the stock and boil until the liquid is reduced to about one-half and has a syrupy consistency. Remove the pan from the heat and add 2 tbsp. (30 mL) soft butter. Pour the sauce over the veal scallops and serve.

ARTICHOKES AND MUSHROOMS

2 tbsp.	butter	30 mL
¼ lb.	mushrooms, sliced	125 g
3 x 14 oz.	cans artichoke hearts	3 x 398 mL
	salt and pepper	
3 tbsp.	soft butter	45 mL

In a skillet, heat 2 tbsp. (30 mL) butter and sauté the mushrooms in it. Cut the artichoke hearts in half, heat them in their liquid, and drain. In a heated serving bowl, combine the artichokes, sautéed mushrooms, seasonings, and the 3 tbsp. (45 mL) soft butter.

CHERRY TOMATOES

2 pints	cherry tomatoes	1 L
⅓ cup	butter	75 mL
1	garlic clove	1
	chopped basil, fresh or dried	
	salt and pepper	

Remove the stem ends from the tomatoes, wash and pat dry. In a heavy pan, melt and slightly brown the butter with the garlic clove. Add the tomatoes and gently sauté until heated through. Remove garlic and season with basil, salt and pepper.

CREAM CHEESE DESSERT

1 lb.	softened cream cheese	500 g
1 cup	sifted confectioners' sugar	250 mL
½ cup	heavy cream	125 mL
2	egg yolks	2
¼ cup	brandy	50 mL

Beat the cream cheese, sugar, cream and egg yolks until the mixture is light. Stir in the brandy. Pour the dessert into stemmed glasses and chill for 2 hours or more before serving. Serve with Berry Sauce, recipe follows.

BERRY SAUCE

2 cups	raspberries or strawberries, fresh or frozen	500 mL
¼-½ cup	sugar, see below	50-125 mL
1 tbsp.	lemon juice	15 mL
2 tsp.	arrowroot	10 mL
2 tbsp.	Cointreau or Grand Marnier	30 mL
2 tbsp.	finely grated orange rind	30 mL

Cook the berries, sugar (½ cup [125 mL] for fresh, ¼ cup [50 mL] for frozen) and lemon juice until soft, about 5 minutes. For raspberries, transfer to a food mill or sieve and purée. Purée strawberries in a food processor. Mix the arrowroot and liqueur together until smooth. Add to the hot fruit mixture and cook over low heat, stirring constantly until clear and slightly thickened. Add grated orange rind and chill before serving.

2	Sponge Cake layers, recipe follows	2
	Rum Sauce, recipe follows	
	Plain Cheese Filling, recipe follows	
1 cup	Chocolate Cheese Filling, recipe follows	250 mL
6 oz.	jar raspberry or apple jelly	170 mL
2 cups	heavy cream	500 mL
¼ cup	icing sugar	50 mL
1 tsp.	vanilla	5 mL

Split each sponge layer through the middle, so that you have 4 layers. Place the first layer, cut side up, on a serving plate. Sprinkle with ⅓ cup (75 mL) Rum Sauce and spread with half the Plain Cheese Filling. Spread the cut side of the second layer with half the jelly and place the layer, jelly side down, on the first. Sprinkle the top with ⅓ cup (75 mL) Rum Sauce and spread it with the Chocolate Cheese Filling. Place the third layer, cut side up, on the second. Sprinkle it with ⅓ cup Rum Sauce and spread it with the remaining Plain Cheese Filling. Spread the cut side of the fourth layer with remaining jelly and place the layer, jelly side down, on the third. Sprinkle the top with the remaining rum sauce.

Beat the cream until it is stiff, adding the sugar and vanilla as you beat. Frost the top and sides of the cake with whipped cream. Refrigerate the cassata for at least 4 hours before serving.

SPONGE CAKE

4	eggs, separated	4
¼ tsp.	cream of tartar	1 mL
1 cup	sugar (divided)	250 mL
¼ cup	water	50 mL
1 tsp.	lemon juice	5 mL
1 tsp.	vanilla	5 mL
1 cup	cake flour	250 mL
¼ tsp.	salt	1 mL
¾ tsp.	baking powder	3 mL

In a bowl, beat the egg whites with the cream of tartar until they form soft peaks. Then, gradually, add ½ cup (125 mL) sugar and continue to beat them to a stiff meringue. In a separate bowl, beat the egg yolks until they are thick and lemon-coloured. Gradually add ½ cup (125 mL) sugar and continue beating until the egg yolks are thick and light. To the ¼ cup water, add the lemon juice and vanilla. In a third bowl combine the flour, salt and baking powder.

Blend the flour mixture and the liquid mixture alternately into the egg yolk mixture and fold in the egg whites. Pour the batter into 2 ungreased 8" (20 cm) layer cake pans and bake in a preheated oven at 350°F (180°C) for 25 to 30 minutes. Invert the pans and cool the layers for 1 hour before turning them out of the pans.

RUM SAUCE

1¼ cups	sugar	300 mL
1 cup	water	250 mL
2	slices lemon	2
4	slices orange	4
⅔ cup	rum	150 mL

Combine the sugar, water, lemon and orange in a saucepan and bring to a boil, stirring constantly. Boil the syrup gently until reduced to 1⅓ cups. Remove the saucepan from the heat and discard the fruit. Add the rum and stir.

CHEESE FILLINGS

1 lb.	ricotta cheese	500 g
½ cup	icing sugar	125 mL
½ cup	semisweet chocolate bits or chocolate chips	125 mL
¾ cup	chopped mixed candied fruit	175 mL
1 tbsp.	rum	15 mL
1 tbsp.	melted semisweet chocolate	15 mL

Beat the ricotta and sugar together until they are well blended. Stir in the chocolate bits or chips, the candied fruit and the rum. Remove 1 cup of the filling and blend it with the melted chocolate. This makes the chocolate cheese filling.

BISQUE TORTONI

⅓ cup	sugar	75 mL
2 tbsp.	water	30 mL
2 tbsp.	sherry	30 mL
3	egg yolks	3
1 cup	heavy cream	250 mL
⅓ cup	toasted blanched almonds, ground	75 mL

In a small saucepan, mix the sugar and water. Bring this syrup to a boil and boil for 3 minutes. Beat the sherry and egg yolks together until they are thoroughly blended. Pour the hot syrup into the egg mixture in a steady stream, beating constantly. Whip the cream and fold it into the egg mixture.

Arrange 8 individual fluted paper cups in a cake pan. Pour the bisque into the cups, sprinkle with almonds, and freeze for at least 2-3 hours. Peel off the paper cups before serving.

GREECE

Drawing of Attic neck-amphora
in early style with animal motifs
in the Corinthian manner.
Greece, ca 560-550 B.C.
Royal Ontario Museum
972.182.2.

GREECE AND THE
MEDITERRANEAN WORLD

The ancient Mediterranean world was the cradle of Western cuisine. Wall paintings and re- liefs show Egyptians planting and harvesting grains, fruits, and vegetables in great variety; making wine and beer; hunting wild game and birds; and enjoying splendid feasts. In the Egyptian collections of the Royal Ontario Museum is a fragment of a wall relief that depicts a harvest scene, with a charming donkey ready to transport sheaves of wheat from the field.

The oven was invented in the Nile valley and the process of leavening bread was introduced there. Three thousand years ago professional bakers and housewives knew how to make thirty different kinds of breads and cakes.

From the time of the legendary Homeric banquet to the era of sophisticated dining in the later Greek civilization, the Greeks developed cooking into an art, which was carried to even more elaborate heights by the Romans. Writers of the time have described, in lavish detail, recipes that made use of herbs, stuffings and sauces to enhance meats, fish, vegetables and fruits.

The Greeks drank wine not only for pleasure but also to promote religious ecstasy. Dionysus, the god of wine, is represented on many of the vessels in the collections of the Greek and Roman Department. These beautifully decorated objects were all made to be used; the shapes varied according to the intended function. There are containers for oil and for wine, drinking cups and mixing bowls, many painted with lively scenes that provide a very valuable source of knowledge of ancient Greek society. A common motif was the laurel wreath, the crown of victors in the games. The laurel leaf was also used in cooking and is known to us still as the indispensible bay leaf.

Elegant silverware was also used. A lovely silver ladle, with a handle ending in a duck's head, may be seen in the Greek Gallery.

CLASSIC SIMPLICITY

For your Greek meal, evoke the sunny Mediterranean world with a centrepiece consisting of a black pottery comport filled with pomegranates, lemons and ivy leaves. Greek shops carry pottery plates and bowls in black and terracotta. Copper accessories, too, are very suitable for a Greek table. Beige, green, or apricot place mats and napkins made of a rough linen-textured or coarsely woven material, would give the right feeling for this sometimes stark but beautiful land.

Serves 8

Zucchini Casserole
Greek Salad
with Garlic Vinaigrette Dressing
Poached Apples with Whipped Cream
Sugared Shortbread

ZUCCHINI CASSEROLE

8	small zucchini	8
½ cup	butter	125 mL
4	small onions, finely chopped	4
2 tbsp.	chopped parsley	30 mL
1⅓ cups	grated Parmesan cheese	325 mL
2	eggs, beaten	2
4 cups	soft bread crumbs	1 L
	White Sauce, recipe follows	

Cut off the ends of the zucchini, but do not peel them. Cook whole zucchini in boiling water for 5 to 10 minutes, until tender-crisp. Drain the zucchini and set them aside to cool. In a skillet, heat the butter and sauté the onions in it until they are just soft. Remove from heat. Add the parsley, 1 cup (250 mL) cheese, eggs and bread crumbs, and mix thoroughly. Split the zucchini lengthwise and remove a little pulp along the centre of each half. Fill the hollows with the stuffing and arrange the halves, stuffed side up, in a greased baking dish. Pour the White Sauce over the zucchini, sprinkle the remaining cheese over the top, and bake, uncovered, at 350°F (180°C) for 20-30 minutes, or until the top is bubbly.

WHITE SAUCE

4 tbsp.	butter	60 mL
4 tbsp.	flour	60 mL
2 cups	milk, scalded	500 mL
1	egg beaten	1
	salt and pepper to taste	

Melt the butter in a saucepan over low heat. Add the flour and cook until it is bubbly, stirring constantly. Add the milk slowly, beating constantly with a wire whisk. Cook until the sauce is thickened. Remove from heat and whisk in the egg. Season with salt and pepper.

GREEK SALAD

6-8 cups	bite-sized pieces romaine or leaf lettuce	1.5-2 L
1	large cucumber, sliced	1
16	or more pitted Calamata olives	16+
1	Bermuda or red onion, cut into rings	1
2	large tomatoes, peeled and cut into wedges	2
8	or more, anchovy filets, rinsed and patted dry	8+
½ lb.	or more, feta cheese, crumbled	250 g +
	Garlic Vinaigrette Dressing, recipe follows	

Combine all the salad ingredients in a salad bowl. Add Garlic Vinaigrette Dressing to taste and toss gently.

GARLIC VINAIGRETTE DRESSING

1	garlic clove, peeled and halved	1
2 tbsp.	red wine vinegar	30 mL
6-8 tbsp.	olive oil	90-120 mL
¼ tsp.	dried basil or oregano	1 mL
	salt and pepper to taste	

Combine all the ingredients in a bowl, several hours before you plan to use the dressing. Before adding the dressing to the salad, remove the garlic.

POACHED APPLES

2½ cups	water	625 mL
1 cup	sugar	250 mL
¼ cup	lemon juice	50 mL
6	red Delicious apples	6
1 cup	heavy cream, whipped	250 mL
2 tbsp.	brown sugar	30 mL
1 tsp.	cinnamon	5 mL

In a large saucepan, bring the water, sugar and lemon juice to a boil. Pare the apples, cut them in quarters and core them. Place the apples in the syrup in the saucepan. Lower the heat and simmer, covered, until the apples are tender; carefully turn the quarters occasionally to be sure they are coated with syrup. Remove the apples from the pan and place them in a serving dish. Boil the syrup until it is slightly reduced and pour it over the apples. If the poached apples are prepared several hours in advance, refrigerate them. Serve with a bowl of whipped cream that has been flavoured with brown sugar and cinnamon.

SUGARED SHORTBREAD

1 cup	butter	250 mL
½ cup	confectioner's sugar	125 mL
1	egg yolk	1
½ tsp.	baking powder	2 mL
1½ tsp.	salt	7 mL
3 cup	cake flour	750 mL
½ cup	chopped, browned almonds	125 mL
2 tbsp.	Cointreau	30 mL
1 tsp.	vanilla	5 mL
	icing sugar	

Cream the butter, in an electric mixer or food processor if you have one. Slowly add the ½ cup (125 mL) sugar and then the egg yolk and blend thoroughly until the mixture is light coloured. Sift the combined baking powder, salt and flour into the mixture. Mix well. Add the almonds, Cointreau and vanilla, and mix thoroughly. With your hands, shape the dough into balls approximately 1" (2.5 cm) in diameter and place them on an ungreased cookie sheet, well separated. Pat the balls down into rounds about ¼" (6 mm) thick. Bake in a preheated oven at 350°F (180°C) for 15 to 20 minutes, or until the cookies are a delicate beige colour. Remove the cookies from the cookie sheet to a rack and sprinkle them liberally with icing sugar. Makes approximately 5 dozen cookies.

Serves 8

Artichokes à la Grecque
Shrimp and Tomato Casserole
or
Spinach and Cheese in Phyllo Pastry
Salad of Assorted Greens
with Lemon Paprika Dressing
Fresh Fruit and Yoghurt
Orange Squares

ARTICHOKES À LA GRECQUE

3 x 14 oz.	frozen artichoke hearts	3 x 398 mL
¼ cup	olive oil	50 mL
1 cup	water	250 mL
2 tbsp.	vinegar	30 mL
½ cup	chopped parsley	125 mL
2	carrots, diced	2
½	·celery stalk, sliced	½
½ tsp.	minced garlic	2 mL
1 tbsp.	flour	15 mL

Drain and cut artichokes in half. Place all other ingredients, except the flour, in a saucepan and simmer for about 10 minutes. Add artichokes and simmer gently for 5 minutes. Remove artichokes to a shallow dish. Strain 1 cup (250 mL) of the cooking liquid into a saucepan, discarding the solids. Dissolve the flour in a little cold water and stir into the liquid. Bring to a boil, stirring. Pour the sauce over the artichokes and refrigerate. Serve with a spoonful of sauce drizzled over each serving.

SHRIMP AND TOMATO CASSEROLE

¼ cup	olive oil	50 mL
3-4	large onions, chopped	3-4
1	garlic clove, minced	1
2 x 14 oz.	cans Italian tomatoes, with liquid	2 x 398 mL
5½ oz.	can tomato paste	156 mL
¼ cup	butter	50 mL
1 lb.	uncooked shrimp, peeled and cleaned	500 g
2-3 tbsp.	ouzo	30-45 mL
1 lb.	feta cheese*	50 g
¼ cup	chopped parsley	50 mL
1 cup	rice, or 2 cups (500 mL) of orzo**, cooked	250 mL

In a skillet, heat the oil and sauté the onion and garlic in it. Add the tomatoes and tomato paste and simmer for about 30 minutes, or until the mixture is reduced to a sauce. In a pan, heat the butter and sauté the shrimp in it until they are just pink. Pour the ouzo over them and flame. Add the shrimp to the sauce and transfer the mixture to a 2-quart (2 L) casserole.

Crumble the feta cheese over the casserole and sprinkle with the parsley. Bake, uncovered, at 350°F (180°C) for 30 minutes, or until hot and bubbly, and serve over rice or orzo.

*A combination of half feta and half cottage cheese may be used if preferred.

**Orzo is a rice-shaped pasta. Cook according to package directions.

—Spinach And Cheese In Phyllo Pastry—

¼ cup	olive oil	50 mL
1	onion, chopped	1
2 lbs.	fresh spinach or 3 x 10 oz. (283 g) pkgs. frozen spinach, thawed and drained	1 kg
1 cup	chopped parsley	250 mL
¼ cup	chopped fresh dill	50 mL
4	eggs slightly beaten	4
1 lb.	feta cheese, crumbled	500 g
	pepper	
	nutmeg	
1 pkg.	phyllo pastry*	1
½ cup	melted butter	125 mL

In a heavy skillet or saucepan, heat 2 tsp. (10 mL) of the oil and sauté the onion in it until it is limp. Add the spinach and cook until it is just wilted, stirring constantly. Cool the spinach and add the parsley and dill. Mix the eggs, cheese, pepper to taste and a pinch of nutmeg, and add the mixture to the spinach. In a 12 x 8" (30 x 20 cm) greased baking dish, place a sheet of phyllo so that it extends up the sides of the dish. Brush the pastry with melted butter. Add 5 more layers of phyllo, brushing each with butter. Spoon the spinach mixture into the pastry shell. Cover with as many layers of phyllo as the package yields, brushing each layer with butter. For an interesting surface, score a diamond pattern through the top layers. Bake, uncovered, at 375°F (190°C) for 40 to 50 minutes, or until the pastry is golden and puffy.

This recipe may also be used for hors d'oeuvres to serve 16.

*Phyllo can be obtained at a Greek grocery and comes already rolled and paper thin.

SALAD OF ASSORTED GREENS

See recipe page 16.

LEMON PAPRIKA DRESSING

1	lemon, juice and 4 very thin strips of rind	1
1	garlic clove, peeled and crushed	1
1 tsp.	sweet Hungarian paprika	5 mL
1 cup	olive oil	250 mL
	white wine vinegar, to make ⅓ cup (75 mL) combined with lemon juice	
1 tbsp.	sugar	15 mL
½-¾ tsp.	salt	2-3 mL
½ tsp.	dry mustard	2 mL

In a bowl, thoroughly mix all the ingredients and allow to stand for 24 hours. Before adding the dressing to the salad, strain the liquid to remove the lemon rind and garlic.

Orange Squares

2	medium oranges	2
2	eggs	2
1½ cups	firmly packed brown sugar	375 mL
1⅓ cups	all-purpose flour	325 mL
¾ tsp.	baking powder	3 mL
½ tsp.	salt	2 mL
	Orange Icing, recipe follows	

Grate the rind from the 2 oranges. Peel and section the oranges, chop them, and set them aside. In a large bowl, beat the eggs and sugar until well combined. Fold in the flour, baking powder, salt, chopped oranges and rind. Spread the batter in a greased and floured 9 x 13" (23 x 33 cm) cake pan. Bake in a preheated oven at 350°F (180°C) for 25 minutes. Allow to cool. Spread with Orange Icing and cut into squares.

Orange Icing

¼ cup	soft butter or margarine	50 mL
2 cups	confectioner's sugar	500 mL
2 tbsp.	grated orange rind	30 mL
3-4 tbsp.	orange juice, or enough to give the icing a spreading consistency	45-60 mL
	pinch of salt	

In a bowl, cream the butter and gradually add the sugar and the rest of the ingredients. Beat until smooth.

DINNER

Serves 8

Eggplant Salad
Dolmades (Stuffed Grape Leaves)
Lamb Avgolemono
Rice and Nut Pilaf
Watercress and Spinach Salad With Creamy Dressing
Almond Tartlets

EGGPLANT SALAD

2	large eggplants	2
2	garlic cloves, peeled and mashed	2
1	small onion, grated or 4 tbsp. (60 mL) finely chopped scallions	1
2 tbsp.	chopped parsley	30 mL
2	large tomatoes, peeled and chopped	2
2 tsp.	marjoram	10 mL
2 tsp.	fine herbes	10 mL
	salt and pepper	
	olive oil	
½ cup	chopped walnuts (optional)	125 mL
	tomato wedges	
	Greek olives	

Pierce the eggplants several times with a fork. Place them in a baking dish and bake at 350°F (180°C) for 1 hour. Remove them from the oven, let them cool, and peel and chop them. Put the chopped eggplant in a bowl and add the garlic, onion, parsley, chopped tomato, marjoram and fine herbes, and mix well. Add salt and pepper to taste and enough olive oil to moisten the mixture. Add walnuts if desired. Mix well and chill. Serve on a bed of lettuce with tomato wedges and olives.

To use this recipe for a dip, purée the cooked and peeled eggplants in a blender or food processor with all the other ingredients, except the nuts, tomato wedges, and Greek olives. Stir the nuts into the purée and chill it. Serve the purée with melba toast, thinly sliced Greek or French bread, or celery and zucchini sticks.

DOLMADES (STUFFED GRAPE LEAVES)

3 tbsp.	olive oil	45 mL
2 tbsp.	butter	30 mL
1	medium onion, finely chopped	1
½	small garlic clove, crushed	½
¼ cup	chopped parsley	50 mL
2	slices black bread, crumbled	2
½ tsp.	salt	2 mL
¼ tsp.	thyme, dill or mint	1 mL
¼ cup	pine nuts	50 mL
16 oz.	jar vine leaves	500 mL
	lemon juice	
¼ cup	butter, cubed	50 mL

Heat the olive oil and 2 tbsp. (30 mL) butter in a saucepan. Add the onion, garlic, parsley and bread. Stir and sauté. Add the seasonings and nuts and continue to cook gently for a few minutes, but do not brown. Spread out the vine leaves and put a spoonful of the onion mixture on each. Fold over the sides and roll up firmly. Place the dolmades seam-side down in large skillet. Sprinkle them with the lemon juice and dot them with butter cubes. Pour in enough water to come halfway up the dolmades but not cover them. Place a plate on top to weight the dolmades down and simmer for about 10 minutes. Nearly all the liquid will be absorbed. The dolmades are best served cold as an appetizer. Makes about 20.

The stuffing may also be made with a mixture of lean ground beef and bread crumbs. The beef should be sautéed and cooked with the other ingredients and the dolmades should be simmered for about 30 minutes.

3 lbs.	lean shoulder or leg of lamb, boned and cut into 1" (2.5 cm) cubes	1.5 kg
	salt, pepper and minced garlic or garlic powder, to taste	
2 tbsp.	oil	30 mL
2 tbsp.	butter	30 mL
3	onions, chopped	3
2 tbsp.	flour	30 mL
½ cup	water	125 mL
½ cup	white wine	125 mL
2 tbsp.	minced fresh dill	30 mL
2 tbsp.	minced fresh parsley	30 mL
¾ tsp.	salt	3 mL
1	bunch celery, stalks sliced diagonally into 1" (2.5 cm) pieces, and half the leaves chopped	1
2	medium zucchini, sliced diagonally into 2" (5 cm) pieces	2
4	egg yolks	4
6 tbsp.	lemon juice	90 mL
	parsley leaves	

Sprinkle the lamb with salt, pepper and minced garlic or garlic powder. In a large skillet, heat the oil and brown the meat in it. Remove the meat and add the butter and onion to the skillet. Cook the onion over moderate heat until it is wilted. Blend in the flour. Add the water and continue cooking until the mixture is thick and smooth, stirring constantly. Add the wine and stir. Return the meat to the skillet, add the dill, parsley and salt, and simmer, covered, for 1 hour. Add the celery and zucchini and continue cooking 10 minutes. When you are ready to serve, beat the egg yolks in a bowl until they are thick. Beat in the lemon juice, 1 tbsp. (15 mL) at a time. Gradually stir into the bowl 1 cup (250 mL) of the hot liquid from the skillet. Slowly pour the egg mixture into the skillet, stirring until all is well blended. Garnish generously with parsley leaves and serve.

WATERCRESS & SPINACH SALAD
WITH CREAMY DRESSING

See recipes, page 19.

RICE AND NUT PILAF

4 tbsp.	butter	60 mL
6	cloves garlic, crushed	6
2 cups	pine nuts or 4-6 oz. (115-170g) sliced almonds	500 mL
1 cup	raw long-grain rice	250 mL
2	leeks, chopped	2
2-2½ cups	chicken broth	500-625 L
	salt and pepper	

Heat the butter in a skillet and cook the garlic in it for 1 minute. Add the nuts and rice and cook for about 4 minutes, stirring until the rice is lightly browned. Add the leeks and cook for 1 minute. Transfer the mixture to a casserole and add 4 cups (1 L) broth and salt and pepper to taste. Bake at 375°F (190°C) for 1¼ hours, stirring occasionally. Add more broth if the liquid is absorbed before the rice is tender.

1 cup	butter	250 mL
1½ cups	flour	375 mL
½ cup	sour cream	125 mL
3 tbsp.	sugar	45 mL
1 tbsp.	hot water	15 mL
8 oz.	cream cheese	250 g
½ cup	honey	125 mL
¼ cup	chopped toasted almonds	50 mL
8	whole fresh strawberries	8

Cut the butter into the flour with a pastry blender, until the 2 ingredients are thoroughly mixed. (A food processor does the job in seconds.) With a fork, blend in the sour cream. Divide the dough in half, wrap each half in aluminum foil or plastic wrap, and refrigerate for at least 8 hours.

Preheat the oven to 350°F (180°C). Remove 1 package of pastry from the refrigerator and roll it out on a well-floured, cloth-covered board into a circle ¹/₁₆" (1.5 mm) thick. Cut the pastry into 4" (10 cm) rounds. Place 8 rounds on an ungreased cookie sheet and brush each with sugar glaze made by blending sugar and hot water. Roll out the remaining dough and cut it into 4" (10 cm) rounds. Cut a 2" (5 cm) circle out of the centre of each round. Continue to roll and cut the dough until you have 16 rings with empty centres. Place 2 rings on top of each round, 1 at a time. Brush each ring with sugar glaze. Bake at 350°F (180°C) for about 25 minutes, or until the tart shells are light brown. Allow the shells to cool before filling them.

Thoroughly blend the cream cheese and honey and stir in the almonds. Spoon the cheese mixture into the shells and top each tart with a strawberry.

EXOTIC EAST

Drawing inspired by a
lacquer ware picnic set comprising
tiered boxes and two sake decanters.
Decorated with chrysanthemums
and stylized crane crests.
Japan, Edo Period, 18th century.
Royal Ontario Museum
933.35.2.

THE EXOTIC EAST

"You can't take it with you" is a generally accepted philosophy *today, but many early societies* believed that you could, and *made prodigious efforts to do so. In ancient China it was the practice to bury live animals and humans, as well as all kinds of objects, with deceased members of the ruling class to minister to their needs in the afterlife. As civilization advanced, live sacrifice was abandoned and replicas were placed in the tombs. The rich variety and vivid realism of objects found in tombs tell us a great deal about life in China through many centuries.*

In the Han Dynasty (206 B.C. to A.D. 220) craftsman made green-glazed ceramic models of many homely everyday things, such as houses, farm buildings, animals and all kinds of useful equipment. In the collections of the Far Eastern Department there are models of cooking equipment, including grinding mills, braziers with pots and two stoves. Cooking was often done outdoors and the brazier would have been placed near the well. By the later Han period closed stoves were in use. The museum has two delightful examples which remind us of playing house. One has a fish on top, waiting for the pot!

The distinctive character of Chinese cooking was well established by this period. A shortage of firewood had encouraged quick cooking, in contrast to the Western practice of slowly roasting large cuts of meat. The Chinese developed the technique of stir-frying food, which was first shredded or sliced into small pieces. Braziers and stoves like those in the R.O.M. collections were also used for stewing and braising.

Both the Chinese and the Japanese have always been fond of dining out of doors when weather permits. Formal banquets were often held in gardens and pavilions, and picnics have been popular for centuries. An exquisite small picnic basket of lacy carved ivory may be seen in the Later Imperial China Gallery. It is decorated with pastoral scenes and is so delicate that it looks as if it might have been made for a Chinese fairy princess.

In Japan, the "Hanami" or flower viewing is an annual spring activity. The people who flock out to the countryside to see the cherry blossoms carry elaborately prepared picnics as an important part of the ritual. The picnic kits consist of boxes and trays that fit together and contain compartments for different dishes and condiments, and often a rack for sake bottles and cups. In the Japanese collections there are picnic boxes dating from the 17th to the 19th century. They are lacquered and beautifully decorated on the exterior with vegetables, fruits, flowers and leaves. A five-tiered Korean box is inlaid with mother-of-pearl leaves, flowers, fish and crabs. We can hardly imagine packing our more casual picnics in such elegant treasures, although the tiered picnic baskets of rattan and wicker from the Orient found in many of our shops today continue this tradition. They are most attractive and their design is practical both for picnicing and for storage of sewing things.

A Chinese Dinner

Blue and white is the colour scheme that comes to mind for a Chinese dinner. If you own or can beg or borrow blue and white plates, you are well on the way to make-believe Ming effect. Inexpensive dishes can also be found in most Chinese shops; rice bowls are especially attractive and useful for soup, condiments and sauces. Flat woven fans can be used as placemats, with blue or blue and white napkins.

A magnificent centrepiece—and stimulating conversation piece—is a watermelon carved with a dragon pattern.

To carve the melon, first make a paper pattern in the shape of a dragon. Pin it to the green skin with straight pins and draw the outline with a sharp knife. Make a dragon on each side of the melon. Cut away the dark skin carefully to reveal a light green dragon. A red sequin fastened with a pin will give the dragon a wicked flashing eye. Place the melon on a bed of salal leaves and surround it with a circle of rice bowls or lotus bowls, each containing a floating candle. The melon may be hollowed out and filled with fresh fruit for dessert. Add a splash of wine or liqueur, if you wish.

For a larger dragon, increase the graph squares to 1½ inches.

Serves 8

The Three Delicious Soup
Stir-Fried Shrimp with Chinese Vegetables
Spareribs with Kumquats
Beef and Snow Peas
Steamed or Boiled Rice
Stir-Fried Asparagus or Zucchini
Papaya with Lime
Almond Crisps

Most of the recipes for the Chinese Dinner can be cooked in a wok—a fast and healthful way to cook. If you do not have a wok, the recipes can be made successfully in an electric frying pan or a large heavy skillet.

It is essential to have everything prepared before you start to cook. The last-minute cooking can then be accomplished fairly easily. Practise on your family first.

The Chinese use either a dark or a light soy sauce. A happy compromise is the Japanese soy sauce called "Kikkoman".

The main course recipes are designed to serve four people, since this is the largest amount that can be cooked in a wok at one time. The Chinese prefer to serve three or four different main courses at one meal. The recipes given here, served with steamed rice, would be sufficient for dinner for eight people. If only one main course is served, the chosen recipe should be made twice.

1	chicken breast or medium-sized pork chop	1
½ cup	bamboo shoots	125 mL
¼ lb.	fresh mushrooms	125 g
1 tsp.	cornstarch	5 mL
6 cups	chicken stock	1.5 L
1 tbsp.	dry sherry	15 mL
	salt to taste	
1½-2 tsp.	sesame oil	7-10 mL
2	green onions, chopped	2

Skin and bone the chicken breast and sliver the flesh. Roll-cut the bamboo shoots. Sliver the mushrooms. Blend the cornstarch with 2 tsp. (10 mL) of chicken stock, Put the rest of the chicken stock in a pot and bring it to a boil. Add the chicken, bamboo shoots and mushrooms, and simmer, covered, for 5 minutes. Stir in the sherry and salt and then the cornstarch paste. Simmer until the soup thickens, stirring constantly. Pour the soup into 8 bowls and sprinkle a scant ¼ tsp. (1 mL) of sesame oil over each serving. Garnish with chopped green onions.

If you use a pork chop, it is easier to cut up if it is partially frozen. Cut the chop into 2" (5 cm) slivers. After bringing the chicken stock to a boil, add the pork and cook it for 5 minutes, before adding the other ingredients.

STIR-FRIED SHRIMP WITH CHINESE VEGETABLES

4 tbsp.	soy sauce	60 mL
4 tbsp.	sherry	60 mL
10 oz.	can beef broth	284 mL
1 tbsp.	cornstarch, mixed with	15 mL
2 tbsp.	water	30 mL
3 tbsp.	peanut or vegetable oil	45 mL
4	slices ginger, shredded	4
1 lb.	raw shrimp, cleaned and peeled	500 g
10 oz.	can Chinese vegetables	284 mL

In a saucepan, mix the soy sauce, sherry, beef broth and cornstarch paste. Set the saucepan aside. In a deep pot, heat the oil until it smokes. Turn off the heat and let the oil stand for 30 seconds. Turn up the heat, add the ginger and stir-fry for 1 minute. Add the shrimp and continue to cook for 5-7 minutes, stirring constantly. Stir in the Chinese vegetables and pour the mixture into a bowl. Heat the soy sauce mixture until it thickens and pour it over the shrimp and vegetables. This dish may be kept warm in the oven until the other recipes are ready to serve.

4 lbs.	spareribs	2 kg
1/3 cup	soy sauce	75 mL
1/3 cup	chicken broth	75 mL
1/3 cup	dark corn syrup	75 mL
1/3 cup	sherry	75 mL
4	garlic cloves, crushed	4
1 tsp.	ginger	5 mL
1 tsp.	dry mustard	5 mL
1 tsp.	paprika	5 mL
9 oz.	bottle preserved kumquats, sliced	256 mL

Place the spareribs on a rack in a flat roasting pan. Roast at 325°F (160°C) for 1¼ hours. Meanwhile, combine the soy sauce, chicken broth, corn syrup, sherry, garlic, ginger, mustard and paprika in a saucepan and simmer for 3 to 4 minutes. Set the saucepan aside. When the meat is done, remove it from the pan and cut it into individual ribs. Pour off the fat from the roasting pan and return the ribs to it, without the rack. Spoon the sauce over the ribs, coating them thoroughly. Bake at 375°F (190°C) for 40 minutes, basting and turning the ribs occasionally. Add the kumquats and the syrup in the bottle and bake for 10 minutes more.

BEEF AND SNOW PEAS

1 lb.	top round steak, ½" (1 cm) thick	500 g
2 tbsp.	cornstarch	30 mL
2 tbsp.	soy sauce	30 mL
4 tbsp.	vegetable oil	60 mL
½ lb.	snow peas	250 g
1 tsp.	salt	5 mL

Trim all the fat from the steak. Cut it in very thin strips across the grain. Put the meat in a bowl. Sprinkle it with the cornstarch and toss until well-mixed. Pour the soy sauce and 1 tbsp. (15 mL) of the oil over the meat and stir to blend.

Wash the snow peas and trim off ends. In a skillet or wok, heat 1 tbsp. (15 mL) of oil until it is very hot. Add the snow peas and cook over high heat for 1 minute, stirring briskly. Lift out the peas with a slotted spoon and keep them warm.

Add the remaining 2 tbsp. (30 mL) of oil to the skillet and heat until very hot. Add the meat and cook it at high heat for 1 minute, stirring briskly. Sprinkle in the salt and return the peas to the skillet. Cook quickly for 30 seconds, just long enough to heat the peas, stirring constantly. Serve immediately.

STIR-FRIED ASPARAGUS OR ZUCCHINI

1 lb.	fresh asparagus or zucchini, about 3 cups (750 mL) when cut up	500 g
2 tbsp.	oil	30 mL
1 tsp.	salt	5 mL
½ tsp.	sugar	2 mL
1 tbsp.	water	15 mL

Wash the asparagus and drain it well. Cut the tender part into 1" (2.5 cm) roll-cuts and discard the tough part. Set asparagus aside. If you use zucchini, brush them under running water with a vegetable brush. Cut off the ends and slice the zucchini into 1" (2.5 cm) chunks. Preheat the wok for 30 seconds. Add the oil. Add the vegetables and cook for 2 minutes, stirring constantly. Add the salt and sugar and sprinkle about 1 tbsp. (15 mL) of water over the vegetables. Continue cooking and stirring for another 2 minutes. If the vegetables are not tender enough, add 1 more tbsp. (15 mL) of water, cover the wok, and let the vegetables steam for 1 minute. Serve hot.

ALMOND CRISPS

1 cup	butter, softened	250 mL
¾ cup	sugar	175 mL
½ tsp.	salt	2 mL
1	egg, separated	1
1¾ cups	flour	425 mL
1 tsp.	vanilla	5 mL
½ cup	slivered almonds	125 mL

Cream the butter and blend in the sugar, salt, egg yolk, flour and vanilla. Beat the egg white lightly. Press the dough evenly into a ungreased jellyroll pan and paint the surface with the egg white. Sprinkle the nuts evenly over the top. Bake in a preheated oven at 325°F (160°C) for about 40 minutes, or until the edges are light brown. Cut into 1 x 1½" (2.5 x 3.5 cm) bars while still warm. Makes about 4 dozen squares.

Serves 8

Flower Vegetable Soup
Toasted Pita Bread with Curry Butter
Oriental Chicken Salad
Caramel Bananas Flambé
Sesame Seed Cookies

FLOWER VEGETABLE SOUP

2 tsp.	tiny cauliflower florets	10 mL
2 tsp.	thin rounds of baby carrots	10 mL
2 tsp.	thinly sliced green onion	10 mL
2 tsp.	very finely chopped parsley	10 mL
6-8 cups	clear chicken broth	1.5-2 L

Mix the raw vegetables in a bowl. Heat the broth to boiling point. Place 1 tsp. (5 mL) of the raw vegetable mixture in each of 8 bowls. Pour the hot broth over the vegetables and serve.

TOASTED PITA WITH CURRY BUTTER

4-6	pita bread rounds	4-6
	Curry Butter, recipe follows	

Cut rounds of pita bread into pie-shaped wedges and gently pull the pieces apart. Spread the inside of each piece with curry butter and place on a cookie sheet. Toast in a preheated oven at 350°F (180°C) until brown. Store leftover toast in an air-tight container.

CURRY BUTTER

¾ cup	butter, at room temperature	175 mL
	curry powder to taste	

Thoroughly combine the butter and curry powder.

4	whole chicken breasts	4
1 or 2	English cucumbers, depending on size	1 or 2
8	small carrots cut into thin strips	8
6	green onions, very thinly sliced	6
8 tsp.	finely chopped preserved ginger	40 mL
	Ginger Dressing, recipe follows	

Poach the chicken breasts for about 30 minutes, or until they are tender. Remove the bones and cut the chicken into thin strips 3-4" (7-10 cm) long. Peel 1 cucumber, seed it, and cut it into thin strips 3-4" (7-10 cm) long. (If using one large cucumber, reserve enough, unpeeled, for garnish.) Leave the other unpeeled and slice it thinly to use as a garnish. Arrange the chicken on a bed of lettuce on a platter. Intersperse the peeled cucumber and carrot strips with the chicken. Place the unpeeled cucumber slices over the top. Scatter the green onion and chopped ginger over the whole. Pour dressing, to taste, over the salad and serve the remainder in a separate bowl.

GINGER DRESSING

¼ cup	soy sauce	50 mL
½ cup	peanut oil	125 mL
¼ cup	malt or red wine vinegar	50 mL
½ cup	preserved ginger syrup	125 mL

Thoroughly combine all the ingredients in a bowl.

CARAMEL BANANAS FLAMBÉ

¼ cup	butter	50 mL
¼ cup	sugar	50 mL
8	firm bananas, cut in half, across; then in fourths, lengthwise	8
1 tbsp.	cinnamon	15 mL
¼ cup	lemon juice	50 mL
¾ cup	light rum	175 mL

In a chafing dish or frying pan, simmer the butter and sugar until the mixture is the consistency of a medium-heavy syrup. Sprinkle the bananas with the cinnamon and lemon juice and add them to the pan. Cook for 5 minutes. Heat the rum, pour it over the bananas, and flame it. Serve immediately.

SESAME SEED COOKIES

½ cup	soft butter	125 mL
1 cup	less 2 tbsp., sugar	220 mL
1	egg	1
2 tsp.	lukewarm water	10 mL
½ cup	sesame seeds	125 mL
2 cups	all-purpose flour	500 mL
1 tsp.	baking powder	5 mL
½ tsp.	salt	2 mL
1 tsp.	vanilla	5 mL

In a bowl, cream the butter and sugar thoroughly. Add the egg and beat until the mixture is light and fluffy. Add the water and ¼ cup (50 mL) sesame seeds, reserving ¼ cup (50 mL) to sprinkle over the tops of the cookies. Add the flour, baking powder, salt and vanilla, and mix well with a fork. Drop the dough from a teaspoon (5 mL) onto ungreased cookie sheets. Flatten the dough with the bottom of a glass or your fingers. Sprinkle the cookies with the remaining sesame seeds and bake for 10 minutes in a preheated oven at 350°F (180°C). Makes 4 dozen cookies.

AN INDIAN DINNER

To create an Indian atmosphere, use an "Indian Print" bedspread as a tablecloth and plain napkins in complementary colours. Your centrepiece could be marigolds, if they are in season, and other flowers to echo the colours in the spread. A few peacock feathers would also lend a nice touch. Brass candlesticks, plates, or bowls of Indian handwork are easily obtainable and if you have a bric-a-brac elephant or two, so much the better.

INDIAN DINNER

Serves 8

Chutney Cheese Spread
Indian Chicken
Rice with Raisins and Cashews
Endive and Avocado Salad with Creamy Dressing
Baked Pineapple
Date Balls

CHUTNEY CHEESE SPREAD

	light cream	
8 oz.	plain cream cheese, at room temperature	250 g
¼-½ tsp.	curry powder	1-2 mL
	chutney, very finely chopped	

Mix enough cream into the cheese to soften it. Add the curry powder and mix well. Shape the cheese into a mound on a serving plate and top it with your favourite chutney. Serve with melba toast or crisp crackers.

INDIAN CHICKEN

4	large whole chicken breasts, split	4
½ cup	chopped onion	125 mL
4 tbsp.	butter	60 mL
2 tbsp.	oil	30 mL
2 tbsp.	coriander	30 mL
1 tbsp.	chili powder	15 mL
1 tbsp.	turmeric	15 mL
1 tsp.	salt	5 mL
½ cup	hot water	125 mL
2 tbsp.	lemon juice	30 mL

Arrange the chicken pieces on waxed paper and sprinkle the chopped onion over them. Let the chicken stand for ½ hour. Melt the butter and oil in a pan or casserole large enough to hold the chicken pieces in 1 layer. Add the coriander, chili powder and turmeric, and cook for 1 minute, stirring to blend the ingredients. Add the chicken and cook for about 5 minutes, turning the pieces until they are well-coated. Add the salt and water, cover and bake at 350°F (180°C) for 30 minutes. When the chicken is ready to serve, sprinkle the lemon juice over it.

RICE WITH RAISINS AND CASHEWS

2½ cups	water	625 mL
1 tbsp.	salt	15 mL
1 cup	raw white rice	250 mL
2	medium onions	2
1 tbsp.	butter	15 mL
1 tbsp.	oil	15 mL
½ cup	raisins	125 mL
½ cup	cashew nuts	125 mL
	salt to taste	

Bring the water to a boil in a large pot and add salt. When water is boiling, slowly add the rice so as not to stop boiling. Cover the pot, lower the heat and cook until all the water is absorbed. While the rice is cooking, peel the onions and slice very thinly. Separate the rings so they will brown evenly. Sauté onions in the butter and oil until lightly browned. Add raisins, cashews and salt. Stir and mix well. Remove from heat, then add to the rice and combine well. May be served hot or at room temperature.

ENDIVE AND AVOCADO SALAD

8	small endives	8
2	avocados	2
	lemon juice	

Wipe the endives with a wet cloth and separate the leaves. Peel and slice the avocados. Place avocados in a bowl and sprinkle with lemon juice. To serve, arrange the ingredients on individual salad plates. Serve with a bowl of Creamy Dressing.

CREAMY DRESSING

See recipe, page 19.

BAKED PINEAPPLE

2	large, top grade pineapples	2
½ cup	light or amber rum	125 mL
2 tsp.	cinnamon	10 mL
2 cups	sugar, or less	500 mL
4 tbsp.	brandy, warmed	60 mL
1 qt.	vanilla ice cream	1 L

With a sharp knife, cut off approximately the top 1½" (4 cm) of each pineapple. Reserve the tops. Remove the pulp carefully, without piercing the outer shell, and discard the central core. Dice the pineapple. In a large bowl, combine the rum, cinnamon, and sugar (since the sweetness of pineapple varies greatly, you may want to add less than 2 cups (500 mL) of sugar). Add the pineapple to the bowl, mix well, and allow the fruit to marinate for at least 1 hour. Refill the pineapple shells with the marinated pulp. Cover each pineapple with waxed paper, tied with string, and bake at 350°F (180°C) for 30 minutes. Remove the string and waxed paper and put the tops back on the shells to take to the table. Remove the tops and flame the pineapple with brandy. Serve the pineapple pulp with vanilla ice cream.

DATE BALLS

1½ cups	pitted cooking dates	375 mL
3 tbsp.	sugar	45 mL
1 tsp.	powdered cinnamon	5 mL
¼ cup	finely chopped pine nuts	50 mL

Steam the dates for 20 minutes, then mash them and put them in a bowl. Add the sugar and cinnamon and mix them well. Shape the mixture into small balls, about 1" (2.5 cm) in diameter. Roll the balls in the pine nuts. Makes about 18 date balls.

ON THE TERRACE

Drawing of wrought iron gates,
North Italian, 17th century.
Royal Ontario Museum
922.5.1.
Gift of Sir Robert Mond.

ON THE TERRACE

Our prehistoric ancestors dis- covered the method of cooking *outdoors over an open fire, a* method that we are still enjoying *and perfecting. Outdoor cooking remains popular because it imparts a special flavour to food that no other method seems to capture. However, it presents a special challenge to the cook, who must learn to build a good fire and then maintain its heat. Today charcoal barbecues are widely used, as are gas barbecues, which make it possible for devotees to practise their skills in winter as well as in summer.*

Not all terrace parties take the form of a barbecue. Often they involve cooking indoors or advance preparation of dishes that are to be served cold. Whatever the menu and the method of preparation, let nature dictate imaginative garnishes to enhance the presentation of a meal. The old standby parsley is far from the only decoration to be found in your garden or in a country field. Boston ivy is very effective, as are cheerful geraniums or delicate Queen Anne's lace — the possibilities are endless.

If you do a lot of outdoor entertaining, you may want to build a collection of colourful pottery and acrylic dishes and serving pieces. Unbreakable drinking glasses, too, are sensible for terrace and poolside use; today you can find very good-looking plastic wine glasses, as well as tumblers. Plastic cutlery is also available in many lovely colours, and paper plates and cups come in an endless variety of designs and colours. If you use paper plates often, you may want to acquire a set of rattan plate holders, which provide stability for the paper plates. Attractive, colourful paper tablecloths and napkins are readily available, but they can be used only once. Why not make a more permanent easily laundered cloth and napkins from a patterned no-iron sheet or length of fabric? Or use straw placemats, which are very attractive for casual dining.

The crowning glory of your outdoor table should be a centrepiece that evokes the mood of the occasion. A weathervane, for example, makes a provocative centrepiece for a barbecue table. Surround its base with a leafy length of vine, or a selection of leaves and flowers to complement your colour scheme. When plant material is not arranged in water, it must be conditioned for a few hours in cool water and then patted dry and set in place just before the guests arrive.

For a terrace luncheon or supper, you might use your watering can, market basket or a low bowl as a container. Twine ivy around the handle and fill the container with an informal bouquet of grasses and field or country garden flowers. Large napkins in assorted colours would complement the flowers.

Serves 8

Spinach Dip
or
Fish Pâté
Flank Steak
or
Salmon Baked in foil
with Egg and Dill Sauce
Parmesan Potatoes
Green Pea or Pasta Salad
Medley of Summer Fruit
in Lime Rum Sauce
Zucchini Cookies

SPINACH DIP

10 oz.	pkg. frozen chopped spinach	283 g
5	medium green onions and tops, chopped	5
1 tbsp.	chopped parsley	15 mL
3 tbsp.	sour cream	45 mL
½ cup	mayonnaise	125 mL
	salt and pepper	

Defrost the spinach and squeeze it dry. Put the spinach, onion and parsley in a food processor and blend until you have a reasonably smooth mixture. Add the sour cream, mayonnaise and salt and pepper to taste, and mix well. Serve the dip with melba toast rounds or crackers.

This mixture may also be used to stuff tomatoes.

3-4 oz.	smoked salmon	85-115 g
5 oz.	plain cream cheese at room temperature	140 g
3 tbsp.	sherry or dry white wine	45 mL
12	pitted ripe olives	12
½ cup	consommé	125 mL
	freshly ground black pepper	

Process salmon, cheese and wine in a food processor or blender until smooth. Remove to a bowl. Coarsely chop 8 of the olives and combine with the mixture. Add pepper to taste. Place in a serving bowl, smoothing the top, and decorate with slices of the remaining olives. Spoon the consommé gently over the mixture to cover and chill until set. May also be made with tinned salmon, tuna fish or crabmeat. Serve with melba toast, see recipe page 57.

2	flank steaks, 1½ lbs. (750 g) each	2

MARINADE

1½ cups	vegetable oil	375 mL
¾ cup	soy sauce	175 mL
½ cup	lemon juice	125 mL
½ cup	cider vinegar	125 mL
2 tbsp.	Worcestershire sauce	30 mL
2 tbsp.	dry mustard	30 mL
2½ tsp.	salt	12 mL
1 tsp.	pepper	5 mL
1½ tsp.	chopped parsley	7 mL
1	garlic clove, peeled and crushed	1

Thoroughly combine all the marinade ingredients in a large glass or ceramic dish. Add the steaks and turn them once or twice to coat them with the marinade. Cover the dish and refrigerate it at least overnight, or for up to 3 days. Turn the steaks in the marinade occasionally.

Drain the meat and barbecue approximately 5 minutes on each side for medium-rare steak. Season with salt and pepper and slice diagonally across the grain in thin slices.

Salmon Baked In Foil
With Egg And Dill Sauce

8	salmon steaks, ¾"-1" (2-2.5 cm) thick	8
1 tsp.	salt	5 mL
½ tsp.	pepper	2 mL
¼ cup	butter, melted	50 mL
⅓ cup	dry vermouth	75 mL
⅓ cup	lemon juice	75 mL
2 tbsp.	chopped fresh dill	30 mL
2 tbsp.	chopped green onion	30 mL
	Egg and Dill Sauce, recipe follows	

Place the salmon steaks on double sheets of heavy-duty aluminum foil. In a bowl, thoroughly combine the salt and pepper, butter, vermouth, lemon juice, dill and green onion. Pour some of the mixture over each steak. Fold up the foil to make a tightly wrapped package. Barbecue over medium heat for about 35 minutes, or until the fish can be flaked easily with a fork. Serve with Egg and Dill Sauce, recipe follows.

Egg And Dill Sauce

4 tbsp.	butter	60 mL
4 tbsp.	flour	60 mL
1 tsp.	salt	5 mL
2 cups	milk or light cream	500 mL
3-4	hard-cooked eggs, chopped	3-4
¼ cup	chopped fresh dill	50 mL

In the top of a double boiler, melt the butter and gradually add the flour and salt, stirring until the mixture is smooth. Slowly add the milk or cream, stirring constantly to avoid lumps. Cook until the sauce is thickened. Add the chopped eggs and dill. If you want a thinner sauce, add some of the liquid from the fish package.

PARMESAN POTATOES

	butter	
8	medium potatoes, peeled, cut in small cubes	8
	pepper	
	celery salt	
	onion salt	
	Parmesan cheese	

Butter a generous piece of aluminum foil and place the potatoes on it. Sprinkle them with the seasonings and dot them generously with butter. Sprinkle the cheese over them. Fold up the foil, place the package on a second piece of foil, and wrap again. Place the package on a grill and cook for about 30-40 minutes.

GREEN PEA SALAD

4 cups	frozen small peas	1 L
½ cup	vegetable oil	125 mL
2 tbsp.	red wine vinegar	30 mL
1 tbsp.	chopped fresh mint, or 1 tsp. (5 mL) dried	15 mL
½ tsp.	salt	2 mL
6	green onions, thinly sliced	6
2	stalks celery, thinly sliced	2
2	pears, cored and chopped	2
	Mustard Dressing, recipe follows	
	lettuce leaves	

Place the frozen peas in a colander and hold them under the hot water tap. Let the water run as hot as possible until the peas are just thawed. Rinse the peas with cold water and turn them out onto paper towels. When the peas are dry, put them in a bowl. In another bowl, thoroughly combine the oil, vinegar, mint and salt. Pour the mixture over the peas and toss to coat them well. Cover the bowl and refrigerate overnight.

Remove the bowl from the refrigerator. Add the onion, celery and pear, and mix. Pour the dressing over the salad and toss gently. Line a salad bowl with lettuce leaves and turn the salad into it.

MUSTARD DRESSING

½ cup	mayonnaise	125 mL
1 tsp.	lemon juice	5 mL
1 tsp.	Dijon-style mustard	5 mL
1 tsp.	freshly ground pepper	5 mL

Thoroughly combine all the ingredients in a bowl.

PASTA SALAD

1 lb.	green beans, cut into bite-sized pieces, or	500 g
	1 lb. (500 g) broccoli, cut into small florets	
4	medium carrots, in julienne strips	4
½ lb.	fresh pasta (perhaps rotini)	250 g
3 tbsp.	olive oil	45 mL
1	medium sweet red pepper, in thin strips	1
	Garlic Mustard Dressing, recipe follows	
	salt and pepper	
	thinly sliced green onion or chopped chives	

Cook the beans or broccoli, until just tender. Cook the carrots separately until they are just tender-crisp. Boil the pasta in 2 quarts (2 L) of water for 3-4 minutes or until it is al dente. Drain the pasta and put it in a salad bowl. Add the olive oil and toss. Let the pasta cool to room temperature. Add the cooked vegetables and the red pepper and toss. Cover and refrigerate until serving time. Before serving, add the dressing and salt and pepper if desired, and toss thoroughly. Garnish with green onions or chives.

GARLIC MUSTARD DRESSING

1	egg	1
1	lemon, juice of	1
2 tsp.	Dijon-style mustard	10 mL
1 tsp.	salt	5 mL
½ tsp.	pepper	2 mL
½ tsp.	oregano	2 mL
½ cup	vegetable oil	125 mL
1	garlic clove	1

Place all the ingredients except the garlic in a bowl and combine thoroughly with a wire whisk, or blend in a food processor or blender. Add the garlic clove, but remove it before using the dressing.

| 10 cups | fresh fruit | 2.5 L |
| | Lime-Rum Sauce, recipes follows | |

Prepare a selection of whatever fresh fruits are at their best and combine them in a large serving bowl. Pour the sauce over the fruit, mix gently and refrigerate for at least 2 hours.

LIME-RUM SAUCE

1	generous sprig fresh mint	1
⅔ cup	sugar	150 mL
⅔ cup	fresh lime juice	150 mL
1 tsp.	grated lemon rind	5 mL
½ cup	light rum	125 mL

In a bowl, crush the mint thoroughly with the sugar, using a spoon. Add the lime juice and stir until the sugar is dissolved. Add the lemon rind and rum and stir again.

2½ cups	all-purpose flour	625 mL
2 tsp.	baking powder	10 mL
1 tsp.	cinnamon	5 mL
½ tsp.	salt	2 mL
¾ cup	butter or margarine, at room temperature	175 mL
1½ cups	sugar	375 mL
1	egg	1
1 tsp.	vanilla	5 mL
1½ cups	shredded unpeeled zucchini	375 mL
¾-1 cup	coarsely chopped unblanched almonds	175-250 mL
1 cup	semi-sweet chocolate chips	250 mL
	icing sugar	

Sift the flour, baking powder, cinnamon and salt into a mixing bowl. In another bowl, cream the butter and sugar. Beat in the egg and vanilla and stir in the zucchini. Add the dry mixture to this bowl about half at a time, and combine well. Mix in the almonds and chocolate chips.

Drop the mixture a heaping teaspoonful at a time onto a well-greased cookie sheet, keep the spoonfuls about 1" (2.5 cm) apart. Bake in a preheated oven at 350°F (180°C) for 15 to 18 minutes, or until the cookies are lightly browned. Icing sugar may be sifted over the tops when the cookies are cool. Makes about 7 dozen cookies.

TERRACE LUNCHEON OR SUPPER

Serves 8

Chilled Cream of Tarragon Soup
Cold Filet of Beef on a Bed of Aspic
Layered Salad
Hot Buttered French Bread

or

Chilled Pea Soup
Patio Chicken Wings
Salad of Assorted Greens with
Mint Vinaigrette Dressing
Coffee Angel Cake with Coffee Icing

CHILLED CREAM OF TARRAGON SOUP

3 tbsp.	butter	45 mL
1 cup	diced onion or leek	250 mL
3 cups	chicken stock	750 mL
1 cup	peeled and diced potato	250 mL
½ cup	chopped fresh tarragon	125 mL
¼ tsp.	ground nutmeg	1 mL
2 cups	cream	500 mL
1 tsp.	lemon juice	5 mL
	salt and pepper	
8	sprigs tarragon	8

In a heavy-bottomed pot, melt the butter and sauté the onion or leek until it is clear. Add the chicken stock, potato, ¼ cup (50 mL) of the chopped tarragon and nutmeg. Stir until the ingredients begin to simmer. Continue to simmer until the potatoes are soft, about 15 minutes. Add the remaining chopped tarragon and blend or process until the mixture is smooth. Add the cream, lemon juice, and salt and pepper to taste. Mix well and chill. Serve garnished with sprigs of tarragon. Leftover soup freezes well.

COLD FILET OF BEEF ON A
BED OF ASPIC

4-5 lbs.	beef filet	2-2.5 kg
	Aspic, recipe follows	

Cook the beef filet to your taste. Let it cool and slice it.

ASPIC

2 tbsp.	plain gelatin (2 x 7 g env.)	30 mL
3½ cups	beef consommé, stock or bouillon	875 mL
½ cup	port or Madeira	125 mL

Soften the gelatin in a little cold consommé. Put the consommé in a saucepan over moderate heat and blend in the gelatin, stirring until it is completely dissolved. Add the wine and stir.

Pour 2 cups (500 mL) of the liquid into a metal bowl and stir over ice until it is on the point of setting. Arrange the sliced beef on a platter, spoon the 2 cups (500 mL) of partly set aspic over it, and refrigerate. If you prefer a thicker coat of aspic, remove the platter from the refrigerator after 10 or 15 minutes (when the first layer should be set) and coat again. Refrigerate to set the second layer.

Chill the remaining gelatin mixture until it is thoroughly set. Cut the aspic into small cubes and arrange them around the meat on the platter.

1	medium head lettuce, finely shredded	1
3	large carrots, grated	3
2 tbsp.	finely chopped green pepper	30 mL
1	English cucumber or zucchini, thinly sliced	1
1	red-skinned onion, thinly sliced	1
10 oz.	Swiss cheese, finely shredded	285 g
10 oz.	pkg. frozen green peas	285 g
	Creamy Herb Dressing, recipe follows	
10	strips bacon, cooked crisp, crumbled	10

Place a layer of lettuce on the bottom of a deep clear glass bowl. Add a layer of each of the vegetables, and then a layer of cheese. Repeat the layers until all the cheese and vegetables are used up. Use the peas for the top layer of the salad. Pour the dressing over the salad, making sure it covers the top and seeps down the sides. Refrigerate the salad overnight. Just before serving it, sprinkle the top with the crumbled bacon.

CREAMY HERB DRESSING

1 cup	mayonnaise	250 mL
1 cup	sour cream	250 mL
1 tbsp.	sugar	15 mL
½ tsp.	dill	2 mL
½ tsp.	marjoram	2 mL
½ tsp.	thyme	2 mL
½ tsp.	salt	2 mL
½ tsp.	pepper	2 mL

Thoroughly combine all the ingredients in a bowl.

CHILLED PEA SOUP

5 cups	chicken stock	1.25 L
1	small onion stuck with 2 cloves	1
1	small garlic clove, peeled	1
2 tbsp.	fresh tarragon, or 1 tsp. (5 mL) dried	30 mL
3 x 10 oz.	pkgs. frozen peas	3 x 283 g
	salt and pepper	
1 cup	heavy cream	250 mL
1 cup	light cream	250 mL

Put the chicken stock in a large saucepan. Add the onion, garlic, tarragon and peas. Cook until the peas are just tender. Remove the saucepan from the stove and discard the onion and garlic. Purée the mixture until it is smooth. Add salt and pepper to taste and the creams. Mix thoroughly and chill.

PATIO CHICKEN WINGS

40-48	chicken wings	40-48

MARINADE

2 cups	chicken stock	500 mL
2 cups	soy sauce	500 mL
1 cup	pale dry sherry	250 mL
2	medium garlic cloves, peeled and minced	2

Remove the tips of the chicken wings and arrange the wings in a flat dish. In a bowl, thoroughly combine all the marinade ingredients. Pour the marinade over the chicken wings; it should cover them. Marinate overnight in the refrigerator. Cook the wings on a barbecue for approximately 20 minutes, or until they are golden brown. Turn them frequently while they are cooking and baste them with marinade after each turning.

SALAD OF ASSORTED GREENS

See recipe, page 16.

MINT VINAIGRETTE DRESSING

See recipe, page 59.

COFFEE ANGEL CAKE

1	angel food cake mix	1
3 tbsp.	instant coffee powder	45 mL
	Coffee Icing (recipe follows)	

Blend the coffee powder into the dry cake mix and then make the cake according to the directions on the package. Cool before frosting. Frost the entire cake with the icing and decorate it with the almonds.

COFFEE ICING

2 cups	confectioner's sugar	500 mL
2 tbsp.	instant coffee powder	30 mL
1	egg, slightly beaten	1
2 tbsp.	soft butter	30 mL
3 tbsp.	light cream	45 mL
1 cup	thinly sliced almonds	250 mL

Put all the ingredients except the almonds in a bowl. By hand, or with an electric mixer, beat them until you have a smooth, soft icing. Add more cream if necessary.

A ROMANTIC EVENING

A romantic evening calls for a more formal setting and the glow of many flickering votive candles. A few insect-repelling candles are a thoughtful touch — your guests may not be as fond of bugs as is the Museum Department of Entomology. Strings of little white or clear Christmas lights outlining the terrace railing lend an ethereal touch. A low bowl with candles, tuberous begonia, clematis, full-blown roses, or impatiens floating on the water is very effective. Packages of flat floating candles are available at gift and flower shops.

For a somewhat more ambitious centrepiece you might like to try your hand at topiary. A single tree or a pair can be very effective and they are not hard to make.

Line a flower pot with aluminum foil. Spoon in plaster of Paris and mix with water until thick. Insert a bamboo stake or a straight branch of a height to suit your eye and the container. Let the plaster set well. Make two ball shapes of oasis (a water-absorbent florist's foam), one slightly smaller than the other and cover with chicken wire. Drive a long thin finishing nail through the stake or branch where the bottom of the larger ball will rest. The nail should project at least a half inch on either side. Gently work the lower ball down to the nail. Drive another nail to support the upper ball, and work ball into position. The stake or branch should only go halfway through this ball. Cover each ball with Spanish or sheet moss and keep in place where necessary with wire pins. Wet thoroughly. Insert greens and flowers of your choice around the entire ball shaping as you go. Gently mist with water to keep fresh. Cover the set plaster with moss.

A topiary tree can, of course, be made with one ball only, or if you like the work, with three balls!

A Romantic Evening

Serves 8

Crabmeat Appetizer
or
Minted Watermelon Bells
Barbecued Boneless Loins of Lamb
with Mint Relish
Snowpeas with Carrots
New Potatoes with Lemon and Parsley
Orange Chiffon Mousse
or
Heavenlies
Coconut Cookies

Crabmeat Appetizer

5 oz.	crabmeat	127 g
½ cup	mayonnaise	125 mL
½ cup	chili sauce or ketchup	125 mL
1 tsp.	dry mustard	5 mL
1	small clove garlic, peeled and crushed	1
1 tsp.	horseradish	5 mL
1 tsp.	Worcestershire sauce	5 mL
½ tsp.	Tabasco sauce	2 mL
½ tsp.	salt	2 mL
2	hard-cooked eggs, finely chopped	2

Drain the crabmeat and flake it into a bowl. Add the other ingredients and mix thoroughly. Serve the crabmeat with biscuits or celery sticks.

Minted Watermelon Balls

6 lbs.	watermelon (½ an average watermelon)	2.5 kg
¼ cup	loosely packed, chopped fresh mint	50 mL
8	sprigs fresh mint	8

With a melon baller, cut the fruit into balls and remove the seeds. Put the melon balls in a bowl, add the chopped mint, and mix gently but thoroughly. Refrigerate for at least 2 hours. Serve the melon balls in sherbet glasses, each one decorated with a sprig of mint.

BARBECUED BONELESS LOINS OF LAMB

2 lbs.	boneless lamb loins (2 pkgs. frozen loins)	1 kg
¾ cup	oil	175 mL
¼ cup	fresh lemon juice	50 mL
1 tbsp.	Dijon mustard	15 mL
2	garlic cloves, minced	2
1 tsp.	salt	5 mL
	freshly ground pepper	
1 tbsp.	snipped fresh rosemary, or 1 tsp. (5 mL) dried	15 mL

Thaw loins and mix remaining ingredients for marinade. Arrange meat in one layer in a shallow dish and add marinade. Cover and refrigerate for several hours or overnight, turning occasionally. Remove from refrigerator half an hour before cooking. Barbecue the loins over medium hot coals 4 minutes a side for pink lamb, brushing several times with the liquid. Loins may also be oven-broiled.

MINT RELISH

See recipe, page 168.

SNOW PEAS AND CARROTS

¾ lb.	snow peas, trimmed	340 g
10-12	medium carrots, peeled and cut into julienne strips	10-12
	butter	
	salt and pepper	

Cook the carrots until they are just tender. In a separate pot, bring the snow peas to a boil and cook ½-1 minute. Drain the vegetables and combine them in a serving bowl. Add butter, salt and pepper to taste and mix gently.

NEW POTATOES WITH LEMON AND PARSLEY

24	small new potatoes	24
6-8 tbsp.	butter	90-120 mL
1 tbsp.	lemon juice	15 mL
2	lemons, grated rind of	2
½ cup	chopped fresh parsley	125 mL

Scrape the potatoes and cook them in boiling salted water until they are tender. Melt the butter and add the other ingredients to it. Drain the potatoes and put them in a serving bowl. Pour the butter mixture over the potatoes and toss gently to coat well.

Orange Chiffon Mousse

2	eggs, separated	2
⅛ tsp.	salt	0.5 mL
6 oz.	can frozen orange juice	170 mL
¾ cup	sugar	175 mL
1 tbsp.	unflavoured gelatin (7 g pkg.), softened in	15 mL
½ cup	cold water	125 mL
1 cup	heavy cream	250 mL
	kiwi slices or strawberries (optional)	

Put the egg yolks, salt and orange juice in the top of a double boiler and beat with a whisk until the mixture is light. Gradually beat in ½ cup (125 mL) sugar and the softened gelatin. Continue to beat the mixture over boiling water until it thickens. Remove the pan from the heat and let the custard cool. Beat the egg whites until they are stiff. Whip the cream, adding the remaining ¼ cup (50 mL) of sugar to it. Fold the egg whites and the cream into the custard. Pour the mousse into a serving dish, or into a mould that has been rinsed in cold water and dried or sprayed with vegetable oil. Chill the mousse until it is firm. If you have used a mould, unmould the mousse onto a serving dish. Garnish the mousse generously with kiwi fruit or strawberries.

Heavenlies

1 qt.	vanilla ice cream	1 L
¾ cup	Grand Marnier	175 mL
2	squares semisweet chocolate	2

Slightly soften the ice cream and add the Grand Marnier to it. Beat or process the mixture until it is the consistency of a milk shake. Pour the liquid into stemmed glasses. Shave the chocolate over the top of each glass. Serve with short wide straws.

½ cup	butter	125 mL
1 cup	sugar	250 mL
2 tsp.	baking powder	10 mL
1½ cups	shredded coconut	375 mL
1¼ cups	rolled oats (old-fashioned variety)	300 mL
1	egg white, slightly beaten	1

In a mixing bowl, cream the butter and sugar. Add all the other ingredients and mix thoroughly. Drop the batter a teaspoonful at a time onto a greased cookie sheet. Keep the teaspoonfuls of batter well separated, since the cookies will spread. Bake in a preheated oven at 350°F (180°C) for 10 minutes, or until the cookies are lightly browned. Let the cookies stand for a few seconds to harden a little, because they are difficult to lift from the cookie sheet. Makes 1½-2 dozen cookies.

Serves 8

Cream of Corn Soup
Pork Tenderloin
Pasta with Butter and Herbs
Chard Salad with French Dressing
Fruit and Cheddar Cheese
Fudge Squares

CREAM OF CORN SOUP

3 tbsp.	butter	45 mL
1	medium onion, sliced	1
½ cup	35% cream (whipping cream)	125 mL
2 x 14 oz.	tins cream-style corn	2 x 398 mL
2 cups	chicken stock	500 mL
1 cup	milk	250 mL
1 cup	light cream	250 mL
1½ tsp.	salt	7 mL
	chopped parsley and chives	

Melt butter and gently sauté onion until soft but not brown. Add 35% cream, bring to the boil and gently cook until slightly thickened. Transfer to a food mill or strainer, add the corn and process. Stir in the stock, milk, cream and salt. Serve hot or cold, sprinkled with the chopped parsley and chives.

4	pork tenderloins, ¾-1 lb. (365-500 g) each	4

MARINADE

3 tbsp.	ground coriander	45 mL
½ cup	vegetable oil	125 mL
¼ cup	sugar	50 mL
4	garlic cloves, peeled and crushed	4
2 cups	chopped onion	500 mL
½ cup	soy sauce	125 mL
½ cup	lemon juice	125 mL
¼ tsp.	Tabasco sauce	1 mL

Thoroughly combine all the marinade ingredients in a dish. Add the tenderloins. Cover the dish and refrigerate for 5 to 6 hours, or overnight. Barbecue the tenderloins for approximately 10 minutes on each side, with the rack 5"-6" (13-15 cm) above the heat. While the meat is cooking, simmer the marinade on the stove. Slice the meat on the diagonal and serve it with the marinade.

PASTA WITH BUTTER AND HERBS

16 oz.	fresh pasta	500 g
½ cup	melted butter	125 mL
1 cup	finely chopped fresh herbs of your choice	250 mL
	salt and pepper	

Cook pasta in 5 quarts (5 L) of rapidly boiling water, until the pasta is al dente, 2 to 5 minutes. (If packaged pasta is used, cook according to directions given.) Drain the pasta thoroughly and place in a heated bowl. Add the butter, herbs, salt and pepper to taste, and mix lightly.

CHARD SALAD

1 lb.	Swiss chard or spinach, torn into bite-sized pieces	500 g
1 cup	bean sprouts	250 mL
6	green onions, chopped	6
2	hard-boiled eggs, chopped	2
6	slices of bacon, cooked crisp and crumbled	6
1 tbsp.	chopped dill	15 mL
1 tbsp.	chopped parsley	15 mL

Put all the ingredients in a salad bowl and mix them gently. Add 2-3 tbsp. of French Dressing, recipe follows, and toss until all the ingredients are lightly coated.

FRENCH DRESSING

½ cup	wine vinegar	125 mL
⅓ cup	olive oil	75 mL
⅓ cup	vegetable oil	75 mL
¾ tsp.	Worcestershire sauce	3 mL
1½ tsp.	salt	7 mL
½ cup	sour cream	125 mL

With a fork or a wire whisk, thoroughly mix the vinegar, oils, Worcestershire sauce and salt, to make basic French Dressing. Add the sour cream and blend. Store the dressing in the refrigerator.

FUDGE SQUARES

½ cup	butter	125 mL
1 cup	brown sugar	250 mL
1	egg, well-beaten	1
1 tsp.	vanilla	5 mL
1 cup	all-purpose flour	250 mL
1 tsp.	baking powder	5 mL
½ tsp.	salt	2 mL
½ cup	chopped nuts	125 mL

Melt the butter in a saucepan. Add the sugar and stir until it is dissolved. Cool slightly and blend in the egg, vanilla, sifted dry ingredients and nuts. Pour the batter into an 8" (20 cm) square pan and bake in a preheated oven at 350°F (180°C) for about 20 minutes. Ice, if desired, with Brown Sugar Icing, recipe follows. Cut in squares when cool.

BROWN SUGAR ICING

1 cup	brown sugar	250 mL
¼ cup	light cream	50 mL
1 tsp.	butter	5 mL

Combine all ingredients in a saucepan and bring the mixture to a boil. Boil for 3 minutes. Cool slightly and beat. Watch the consistency carefully and be ready to spread the icing quickly, before it gets too stiff.

PARTIES

DINNER PARTY

Unless your dining room is a baronial hall you will probably plan a party for sixteen as a buffet. However, dinner guests are more comfortable seated at tables. Card tables may be set up in advance if you have room, or at the last minute if everything is ready for quick assembly. Hostesses who prefer to entertain in this way often have plywood circles made which will cover a card table and seat six.

This is the moment to use your candelabra on the dining room table. "Mayfair" cups are containers to hold oasis and a candle, which permit you to arrange flowers around any type or size of candlestick. They are available in metal and plastic, white or silver in colour, wherever flower arranging supplies are sold. You can create a stunning arrangement with your candelabra, and smaller ones for your little tables. You may use different cloths and candlesticks for each table if necessary as long as the overall effect is harmonious.

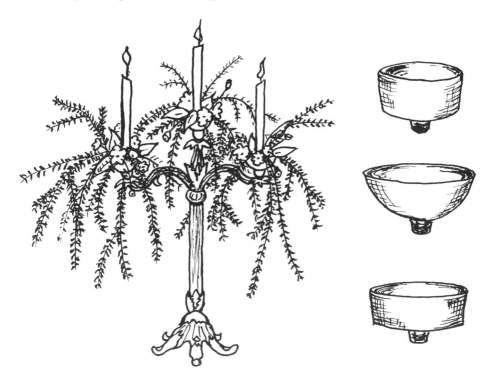

Cheese Log with Melba Toast
(with the drinks)
Baked Chicken Breasts
Rosemary Jelly
Rice Casserole
Puréed Carrots
Chocolate Mint Bombe
with
Marshmallow Fudge Sauce

———————— CHEESE LOG ————————

8 oz.	plain cream cheese	250 g
1½ tbsp.	blue cheese	22 mL
2 tbsp.	butter	30 mL
½ tsp.	Worcestershire sauce	2 mL
½ tsp.	salt	2 mL
1 tbsp.	light cream	15 mL
¾ cup	finely chopped pecans or minced parsley	175 mL

In a bowl combine all the ingredients except the nuts or parsley. Transfer the mixture to a large piece of waxed paper and shape it into a log approximately 2" (5 cm) in diameter. Refrigerate until the log is firm. Roll the log in pecans or parsley. Serve with Melba toast, see recipe page 57, before dinner.

———————— RICE CASSEROLE ————————

2½ cups	raw rice	625 mL
2 cups	chopped celery	500 mL
½ cup	butter	125 mL
4 tbsp.	grated orange rind	60 mL
1½ cups	orange juice	375 mL
3 cups	chicken stock	750 mL
3 tsp.	salt	15 mL

Butter a 3-4 quart (3-4 L) casserole. Combine the ingredients and put into casserole. Cover and bake in a 350°F (180°C) oven for about 1 hour. Stir once or twice with a fork. Mixture should be moist, but all liquid absorbed.

BAKED CHICKEN BREASTS

8	large whole chicken breasts, split, boned, and skinned	8
2 tbsp.	dry mustard	30 mL
2 tbsp.	paprika	30 mL
1 cup	white wine	250 mL
	salt to taste	
½ cup	melted butter	125 mL
2 cups	fine bread crumbs	500 mL

Generously grease 2, 9 x 13" (4 L) casseroles. Shape the half-breasts into rounds and put them in the casseroles, in 1 layer. Combine the mustard, paprika and white wine and drizzle the mixture over the chicken breasts. Sprinkle them with the salt, melted butter and bread crumbs. Bake uncovered at 325°F (160°C) for 1 hour. If the chicken is ready before serving time, cover the casseroles with foil and reduce the oven temperature to 200°F (100°C).

ROSEMARY JELLY

See recipe, page 169.

PURÉED CARROTS

2½ lbs.	carrots	1.25 kg
½ cup	butter	125 mL
1¼ cups	light cream	300 mL
3 tsp.	sugar	15 mL
6 tbsp.	finely chopped parsley	90 mL
4 tbsp.	finely chopped mint	60 mL
	salt and pepper to taste	

Peel carrots and cut into 1" (2.5 cm) pieces. Simmer in water until tender. Drain the carrots and purée in a blender or a food processor. In a large bowl mix the carrots with the remaining ingredients and season to taste. Spread mixture evenly in a buttered baking dish. Place dish in a large pan, adding enough boiling water to come half way up side of dish. Cover with foil for first half hour and bake for 1 hour in a 350°F (180°C) oven.

CHOCOLATE MINT BOMBE

2 qts.	chocolate ice cream	2 L
4	egg whites	4
½ cup	sugar	125 mL
1 tsp.	peppermint extract	5 mL
2 cups	heavy cream, whipped	500 mL
2 cups	finely chopped semisweet chocolate or peppermint candy	500 mL
	green food colouring	

Fill 2, 1-quart (1 L) moulds with all except about 2 cups (500 mL) of the ice cream, leaving the centres hollow to hold the mint filling. With the back of a spoon, smooth the ice cream to spread it evenly in the mould. Place the moulds in the freezer compartment to harden the ice cream. Beat the egg whites until they are stiff, add the sugar gradually, and continue to beat until the egg whites are glossy. Fold in the peppermint extract, whipped cream and candy. Add enough food colouring to tint the mixture pale green. Fill the centres of the moulds with the mint filling and return them to the freezer to allow the bombes to harden. When the centres are firm, cover them with the remaining ice cream. Then cover the bombes with foil and return them to the freezer. Just before dinner is served, remove the bombes from the freezer to the refrigerator. When you are ready to serve dessert, unmould them onto a serving dish.

MARSHMALLOW FUDGE SAUCE

1 lb.	marshmallows	500 g
½ lb.	semisweet chocolate	250 g
1 cup	heavy cream	250 mL
2 tsp.	instant coffee powder	10 mL

Put all the ingredients in a large saucepan and simmer over low heat until the marshmallows are melted, stirring constantly. Serve warm with the bombes.

BUFFET LUNCH

A cheerful and informal centrepiece for the table is ideal for a buffet luncheon.

On a silver-footed platter or gallery-edge tray, arrange a collection of small potted flowering or foliage plants with green apples and pears, artichokes, eggplants, or whatever else takes your eye, to make a pleasing display. Choose linen napkins in various colours to accent or complement the centrepiece.

Cocktail Pecans
Waldorf Chicken Salad
Green Beans Vinaigrette
or
Asparagus, Egg and Mushroom Casserole
Salad of Assorted Greens with French Dressing
Hot Biscuits with Thyme
Butterscotch Crisps
Lemon Curd Cake

COCKTAIL PECANS

1 lb.	pecan halves	500 g
½ cup	butter	125 mL
1 tbsp.	vegetable oil	15 mL
2 tbsp.	brown sugar	30 mL
2 tsp.	ground ginger	10 mL
1 tsp.	curry powder	5 mL
2 tbsp.	chutney	30 mL

Preheat oven to 350°F (180°C).

Spread pecans on a baking sheet and bake for 10 minutes (do not brown). Remove from oven. In a saucepan melt the butter, add the oil, sugar, ginger and curry powder and stir well. Add the pecans and combine with the mixture. Add chutney and mix well. Put mixture back on the baking sheet spread out and return to the oven. Turn oven off and leave for 10 to 15 minutes until dried. Makes about 4 cups (1 L). Store in an airtight container.

8	whole chicken breasts	8
	water	
2-3	green onions chopped	2-3
1-2	celery stalks, with leaves, chopped	1-2
	chopped parsley	
1	bay leaf	1
2 tsp.	salt	10 mL
4	red eating apples, unpeeled, cored and chopped	4
2 cups	finely chopped celery	500 mL
3½ cups	mayonnaise	875 mL
1½ tbsp.	curry powder	22 mL
3 tbsp.	soy sauce	45 mL
	salt and freshly ground pepper	
2 cups	toasted slivered almonds	500 mL
	Boston lettuce	
	watercress	
	seedless grapes	

Place the chicken breasts in a large enough saucepan to hold them comfortably. Add water to cover them by 1" (2.5 cm). Remove the chicken, add 2-3 green onions, 1-2 celery stalks preferably with leaves, some parsley, a bay leaf and 2 tsp. (10 mL) of salt. Bring this to the boil. Return the chicken to the pan, cover and gently poach for 15 to 20 minutes. Remove the pan from the heat and let the chicken cool in the liquid for at least a half an hour. Lift out the chicken, remove the skin and bones and cut the meat into cubes. Put the chicken into a large bowl and add the apple and celery. Mix the mayonnaise with the curry powder and soy sauce and combine with the chicken mixture. Season with salt and pepper to taste. Add more mayonnaise if necessary. Cover and chill for several hours or overnight. Add almonds just before serving. Spoon into 16 nests of Boston lettuce and arrange on a large platter. Garnish with watercress and small clusters of grapes.

GREEN BEANS VINAIGRETTE

See recipe, page 33.

—Asparagus, Egg & Mushroom Casserole—

2 lbs.	mushrooms	1 kg
2-4 tbsp.	butter	30-60 mL
12	hard-boiled eggs	12
5 lbs.	asparagus	2.2 kg
8 cups	milk and mushroom juice	2 L
1 cup	butter	250 mL
1 cup	flour	250 mL
	salt and pepper	
	buttered crumbs	

Slice and sauté mushrooms in butter. Save any juice that accumulates. Shell and slice eggs. Cut asparagus in bite-sized pieces and boil until just tender, about 5 minutes. To make cream sauce, combine mushroom juice with enough milk to make 8 cups (2 L). Melt butter in a large heavy pot, blend in flour and gradually add liquid. Stir constantly, while heating, until the sauce boils and thickens. Season with salt and pepper to taste. Butter 2 casseroles, each large enough to serve 8. Layer eggs, mushrooms, asparagus and sauce, ending with sauce. Top with buttered crumbs. Heat until bubbly in a 350°F (180°C) oven.

This is a flexible recipe which may be divided to serve any number. Proportions of egg, asparagus and mushrooms may be varied if desired.

—————— Salad Of Assorted Greens ——————

See recipe, page 16.

—————— French Dressing ——————

See recipe, page 150.

HOT BISCUITS WITH THYME

4 cups	flour	1L
2 tbsp.	baking powder	30 mL
1½ tsp.	salt	7 mL
4 tbsp.	fresh thyme, or 2 tbsp. (30 mL) dried	60 mL
1 cup	butter	250 mL
2	eggs	2
1 cup	milk	250 mL

Preheat oven to 450°F (230°C).

Combine dry ingredients including the thyme and cut the butter into them with a pastry cutter until texture resembles rolled oats. Beat the eggs with the milk and add all at once to the flour mixture. Mix only until just combined. Drop heaping tablespoons on to greased cookie sheets and bake 10-12 minutes. Serve hot, split and buttered. May be made ahead and frozen. Allow time to thaw, then split, butter and heat in a paper bag in a 350°F (180°C) oven for 5 minutes. Makes 40 biscuits.

BUTTERSCOTCH CRISPS

½ cup	butter	125 mL
1 cup	brown sugar	250 mL
1⅓ cups	quick-cooking oatmeal	325 mL
1⅓ cups	Rice Krispies	325 mL

Melt butter in a saucepan. Add the remaining ingredients and combine well. Spread evenly and gently pat down in a 11 x 16" (28 x 40 cm) cookie sheet with sides. Bake about 12 minutes in a 350°F (180°C) oven. Cool slightly and cut in squares.

LEMON CURD

½ cup	butter	125 mL
½ cup	sugar	125 mL
1	lemon, grated rind and juice	1
1	egg, well-beaten	1

Slowly heat butter, sugar, lemon juice and rind to boiling stirring constantly. Remove from heat and add egg. Beat well to blend. Cool.

CAKE

½ cup	sugar	125 mL
2	eggs, at room temperature	2
½ cup	soft butter	125 mL
1 cup	flour	250 mL
2 tsp.	baking powder	10 mL
	pinch of salt	
2 tbsp.	lemon curd	30 mL
½	lemon, grated rind of	½

Preheat oven to 350°F (180°C).

Mix all the cake ingredients together and beat well. Put into a buttered 8" x 5" (1.5 L) loaf pan and bake 30 to 45 minutes, or until a tester comes out clean. While the cake is baking, make the topping.

TOPPING

1	lemon, juice of, plus rind of ½	1
2 tbsp.	sugar	30 mL

Mix lemon juice, rind and sugar in a saucepan and stir over low heat until sugar is dissolved. Pour over the cake while it is still hot. Cool in the pan.

GIFTS FOR YOUR HOSTESS

Cinnamon Toasted Almonds

Chocolate-Covered Cherries

Candied Grapefruit Peel

Orange Cranberry Bread

Florentines

Maple Lace Wafers

Butter Tarts

Brandied Peaches

Mint Relish

Mustard Pickles

Red Pepper Jelly

Rosemary Jelly

Herb Vinegar

Orange Marmalade

Lemon Paprika Salad Dressing

CINNAMON TOASTED ALMONDS

½ cup	cold water	125 mL
1½ cups	sugar	375 mL
2 tsp.	cinnamon	10 mL
1 lb.	unblanched almonds	500 g

Combine the water, sugar and cinnamon in a saucepan. Simmer over low heat until virtually all the liquid has evaporated. Fold the almonds into the sugar mixture and then spread them evenly on a cookie sheet. Place the cookie sheet about 6-8" (15-20 cm) under the broiler. Keep turning the almonds until they are lightly browned. Remove from heat and allow to cool.

CHOCOLATE-COVERED CHERRIES

4 oz.	semisweet cooking chocolate (4 squares)	115 g
1 oz.	bitter cooking chocolate (1 square)	30 g
1 tbsp.	butter	15 mL
2 tsp.	Grand Marnier	10 mL
2 x 6 oz.	jars maraschino cherries with stems	2 x 188 mL

Melt the chocolate and butter in the top of a double boiler. Add the Grand Marnier and stir. Drain the cherries and dip them one at a time in the chocolate. Place them on waxed paper until the chocolate covering hardens. If the chocolate mixture becomes too cool, it will not stick to the cherries and must be reheated.

When the cherries are cool, put them in individual small pleated paper cups.

CANDIED GRAPEFRUIT PEEL

3	whole grapefruit	3
2 cups	sugar	500 mL
1 cup	water	250 mL

With a spoon, remove white membranes and segment walls from 6 empty grapefruit halves. With a sharp knife, cut the half shells in two. Then, working on the bias, cut even slivers about ⅜" (1 cm) wide and 2" (5 cm) or more long. Place the peel in a large saucepan and cover with cold water. Bring to a boil and drain. Repeat the process 3 times to make rinds pliant and remove excess citrus oil.

Make a syrup of the sugar and water and add the rind to it. Cook over moderately high heat until all but 1 tbsp. (15 mL) of the syrup has been been absorbed, about 20 minutes. Watch carefully for the last few minutes to avoid scorching the rind.

Remove the rind from the syrup, roll in sugar, and spread on sheets of waxed paper to cool and harden.

ORANGE CRANBERRY BREAD

2 cups	all-purpose flour	500 mL
1½ tsp.	baking powder	7 mL
½ tsp.	baking soda	2 mL
½ tsp.	salt	2 mL
1 cup	sugar	250 mL
1	orange, grated rind of	1
¾ cup	orange juice	175 mL
1	egg, beaten	1
2 tbsp.	butter, melted	30 mL
1 cup	raw cranberries, cut in half	250 mL

Combine the flour, baking powder, baking soda, salt and sugar and sift them into a bowl. In another bowl combine the orange rind and juice, egg, butter and cranberries. Stir the liquid mixture into the dry and blend thoroughly. Pour the batter into a greased 9 x 5" (2 L) loaf pan. Bake in a preheated oven at 350°F (180°C) for 50 to 60 minutes, or until a toothpick inserted in the middle of the loaf comes out clean.

FLORENTINES

1 cup	mixed candied peel and cherries	250 mL
½ cup	sultana raisins	125 mL
⅓ cup	almonds	75 mL
½ cup	all-purpose flour	125 mL
¼ cup	butter	50 mL
¼ cup	sugar	50 mL
1 tbsp.	light corn syrup	15 mL
1 tsp.	lemon juice	5 mL
4 oz.	semisweet chocolate (4 squares)	115 g

Chop the peel, cherries, raisins and almonds and put them in a bowl. Add the flour and mix. Melt the butter, sugar and corn syrup in a saucepan. Remove from the stove and stir in the lemon juice and the fruit and flour mixture.

Drop the dough a teaspoonful at a time onto a buttered cookie sheet. Flatten with the bottom of a wet tumbler. Bake in a preheated oven at 350°F (180°C) about 10 to 12 minutes or until the edges are lightly browned. Remove the cookies from the pan and let them cool. Melt the chocolate and ice the bottom of each cookie with it. Makes 24 to 30 cookies, which may be frozen.

MAPLE LACE WAFERS

½ cup	maple syrup	125 mL
¼ cup	butter	50 mL
⅛ tsp.	baking soda	0.5 mL
½ cup	all-purpose flour	125 mL
½ tsp.	baking powder	2 mL
⅛ tsp.	salt	0.5 mL

Combine the syrup and butter in a saucepan and bring to a boil, stirring constantly. Continue to boil for ½ minute. Remove the pan from the heat. Sift the combined dry ingredients into the syrup mixture. Beat briskly. Drop a half teaspoonful at a time onto a greased cookie sheet. Keep the wafers well separated, not more than 8 on a sheet. Bake in a preheated oven at 350°F (180°C) for approximately 6 minutes. Remove the wafers one at a time while they are hot and roll them around a wooden spoon handle to shape them. If wafers become too hard to remove from the sheet, return to the oven long enough to soften for easy removal.

Place them on a rack to cool. Store them in an air-tight container. Makes 40 wafers, but the recipe can be doubled.

BUTTER TARTS

PASTRY DOUGH

See recipe, page 44.

FILLING

1	egg	1
½ cup	raisins	125 mL
½ cup	currants	125 mL
1 cup	brown sugar	250 mL
2 tbsp.	heavy cream or sour cream	30 mL
12	pecan halves	12

In a bowl beat the egg slightly and stir in the fruit, sugar, and cream.

Roll out the dough and cut it to fit the tart tins. Line the tart tins and fill the shells ⅔ full. Put a pecan half on top of each tart and bake in a preheated oven at 375°F (190°C) for 12 minutes, or until the pastry is lightly browned. Cool a bit and remove from the tins to complete cooling. Makes 1 dozen large tarts.

BRANDIED PEACHES

2 cups	sugar	500 mL
3 cups	water	750 mL
6	peaches, peeled	6
4 tbsp.	brandy	60 mL

Put the sugar and water in a large saucepan and cook until the sugar is dissolved. Add the peaches in one layer, bring the syrup to a boil, and boil for about 5 minutes. Remove the peaches to sterilized jars. Boil the syrup about 10 minutes more. Add the brandy and stir. Pour the syrup over the peaches and seal the jars. The brandied peaches should be set aside for 2 weeks to a month for best flavour. Makes 1 quart or 2 pints (1 L).

MINT RELISH

2 cups	sugar	500 mL
2 cups	cider vinegar	500 mL
2 tsp.	dry mustard	10 mL
2 tsp.	salt	10 mL
½ lb.	tomatoes	250 g
1 lb.	red apples, peeled and cored	500 g
1½ cups	seedless raisins	375 mL
1 cup	mint leaves, tightly packed	250 mL

In a saucepan combine the sugar, vinegar, mustard and salt and bring to a boil. Set aside to cool. Put the remaining ingredients through a grinder and add to the saucepan. Bring to a boil again and boil for 3 minutes. Pour the relish into sterilized jars and seal. Let the relish stand for at least 10 days before using. Makes 6 x 8 oz. (250 mL) jars.

RED PEPPER JELLY

12	large sweet red bell peppers	12
6	small hot chili peppers	6
5	lemons	5
8 cups	sugar, warmed	2 L
	white wine vinegar	

Wash the peppers and scrape out all the seeds. Chop the peppers and put them in a large saucepan. Cover them with cold water and bring to a boil. Drain off water. Soften the unpeeled lemons in hot water and then cut them in quarters lengthwise. Remove the seeds from the lemon wedges. Squeeze wedges lightly over the saucepan and then add them to the peppers. Simmer gently for 15 minutes. Let the mixture cool for a few minutes. With kitchen tongs, lift the lemon wedges out of the pan and squeeze all the juice back into pickle mixture. Gradually stir in the sugar. Just cover the mixture with vinegar. Boil for 30 to 40 minutes, or until the mixture begins to gel. Pour the jelly into sterilized jars, and seal the tops with paraffin.

Rosemary Jelly

6½ cups	sugar	1.5 L
2 cups	water	500 mL
1 cup	vinegar (half rosemary vinegar, optional)	250 mL
1 cup	fresh rosemary leaves	250 mL
2	pouches liquid Certo	2
	green food colouring	

In a large saucepan put sugar, water, vinegar and rosemary. Bring to a boil. Remove from heat and steep, covered, for at least 15 minutes. Strain through cheesecloth and discard leaves. Return to large pot and heat to a full rolling boil. Add Certo, boil hard 1 minute. Skim if necessary and add green colouring a few drops at a time until the mixture is an attractive light green. Ladle into sterilized jars and seal. Makes 7-8 x 8-oz (250 mL) jars.

Herb Vinegar

10-12	medium stems mint, tarragon, basil, chives or rosemary (or any other herb of your choice)	10-12
2 cups	red or white wine vinegar	500 mL

Put the herb stems in a pint-size (500 mL) (or larger) jar with a fairly wide mouth. Put the vinegar in a saucepan and bring it just to a boil. Fill the jar with the hot vinegar. If the jar lid is metal, line it with plastic wrap to prevent rust. Seal the jar and let it stand for 2 weeks. Rebottle the vinegar in smaller decorative containers and add a sprig of fresh herb to each bottle. An attractive label provides just the right finishing touch.

Orange Marmalade

See recipe, page 47.

Lemon Paprika Salad Dressing

See recipe, page 99.

MUSTARD PICKLES

6 qt.	basket gherkins, cut in ½" (2.5 cm) chunks	6 L
2 qts.	silverskin onions	2 L
2-3	green peppers, chopped	2-3
2	cauliflower, cut in small florets	2
	coarse pickling salt	

Put all the vegetables in a 3-gallon (15 L) crock, layer by layer, sprinkling salt on top of each layer. Cover and leave overnight. In the morning rinse off salt by filling crock with water, stirring and pouring out into colander. Repeat until water is not salty to taste. Return vegetables to crock.

SAUCE

12 cups	cider vinegar	3 L
2 cups	malt vinegar	500 mL
½ cup	mustard seed	125 mL
½ cup	celery seed	125 mL
12 cups	sugar	3 L
1½ cups	flour	375 mL
1 cup	dry mustard	250 mL
2 tbsp.	turmeric	30 mL
2 cups	malt vinegar	500 mL

Boil the cider vinegar, 2 cups (500 mL) malt vinegar, mustard and celery seed for 20 minutes. Add sugar to the boiling mixture and stir until dissolved. Sift the flour, mustard and turmeric together. Add 2 cups (500 mL) malt vinegar slowly and stir to make a smooth paste. Add the hot sauce a little at a time, stirring constantly to make smooth. Cook the combined mixtures for 10 minutes, pour over the vegetables in the crock while still hot, and stir. Do not put in a cool place until it has cooled. Stir again. Do not use for 2 months. Keeps indefinitely in a cool place.

INDEX

INDEX

INDEX

INDEX

A COOK'S TOUR OF THE R.O.M.

Please send me _____ copies of **A COOK'S TOUR OF THE R.O.M.** at $14.95 per copy, plus $3.00 for shipping and handling, plus 50 cents for additional books.

*After January 1, 1991, the Goods and Services Tax should be added to the total amount of book(s) and shipping and handling.

Name _____

Address _____

City _____ Province _____ Postal Code _____

Telephone Number _____

Please charge to ☐ Visa   ☐ Mastercard   ☐ American Express

Account Number _____ Expiry Date _____

Signature _____

Make cheque or money order payable to ROM Reproductions

ROM Reproductions
Royal Ontario Museum
100 Queen's Park
Toronto, Ontario
Canada
M5S 2C6

U.S. and International orders payable in U.S. funds

- -

A COOK'S TOUR OF THE R.O.M.

Please send me _____ copies of **A COOK'S TOUR OF THE R.O.M.** at $14.95 per copy, plus $3.00 for shipping and handling, plus 50 cents for additional books.

*After January 1, 1991, the Goods and Services Tax should be added to the total amount of book(s) and shipping and handling.

Name _____

Address _____

City _____ Province _____ Postal Code _____

Telephone Number _____

Please charge to ☐ Visa   ☐ Mastercard   ☐ American Express

Account Number _____ Expiry Date _____

Signature _____

Make cheque or money order payable to ROM Reproductions

ROM Reproductions
Royal Ontario Museum
100 Queen's Park
Toronto, Ontario
Canada
M5S 2C6

U.S. and International orders payable in U.S. funds